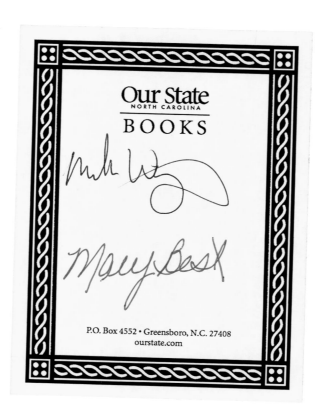

Our State
NORTH CAROLINA
BOOKS

Mike W...

Mary Best

P.O. Box 4552 • Greensboro, N.C. 27408
ourstate.com

North Carolina Churches:
Portraits of Grace

Edited by Mary Best
Photography by Mark Wagoner
Designed by Larry Williams

CONTRIBUTORS
Stories by Mary Best, Deena C. Bouknight, Kathy Grant Westbrook,
David La Vere, Keith McKenzie, Diane Silcox-Jarrett, Jimmy Tomlin,
and Mark Wagoner

Additional photography by Matt Hulsman, Ray Matthews,
Keith McKenzie, Bruce Roberts, Les Todd, and Alan Watson

Map by Jane Shasky

Our State
NORTH CAROLINA
BOOKS

Published by:
Our State Books
P.O. Box 4552
Greensboro, N.C. 27404
800.948.1409
ourstate.com

Printed in China by R.R. Donnelley & Sons.

Publisher: Bernard Mann
Executive Vice President: Lynn Tutterow
Editor and Associate Publisher: Mary Best
Art Director and Designer: Larry Williams
Copy Editors: Amanda Hiatt and Betty Work
Marketing Director: Amy Jo Wood
Production Director: Cheryl Bissett
Distribution Manager: Erica Derr

Photography copyright © Mark Wagoner Productions.
All photos are by Mark Wagoner unless otherwise credited on page 220.

Library of Congress Cataloging-in-Publication Data

North Carolina churches : portraits of grace / edited by Mary Best ;
photography by Mark Wagoner ; stories by Deena C. Bouknight ... [et al.].
    p. cm.
  Includes bibliographical references and index.
  ISBN 0-9723396-4-7 (alk. paper)
 1. North Carolina--Church history. 2. Church buildings--North Carolina.
3. North Carolina--Church history--Pictorial works. 4. Church
buildings--North Carolina--Pictorial works. I. Best, Mary, 1962- II.
Bouknight, Deena C., 1964-
  BR555.N78N67 2004
  277.56--dc22

                    2004016367

Love ...

bears all things,

believes all things,

hopes all things,

endures all things.

Love never ends.
I Corinthians 13:7-8

Table of Contents

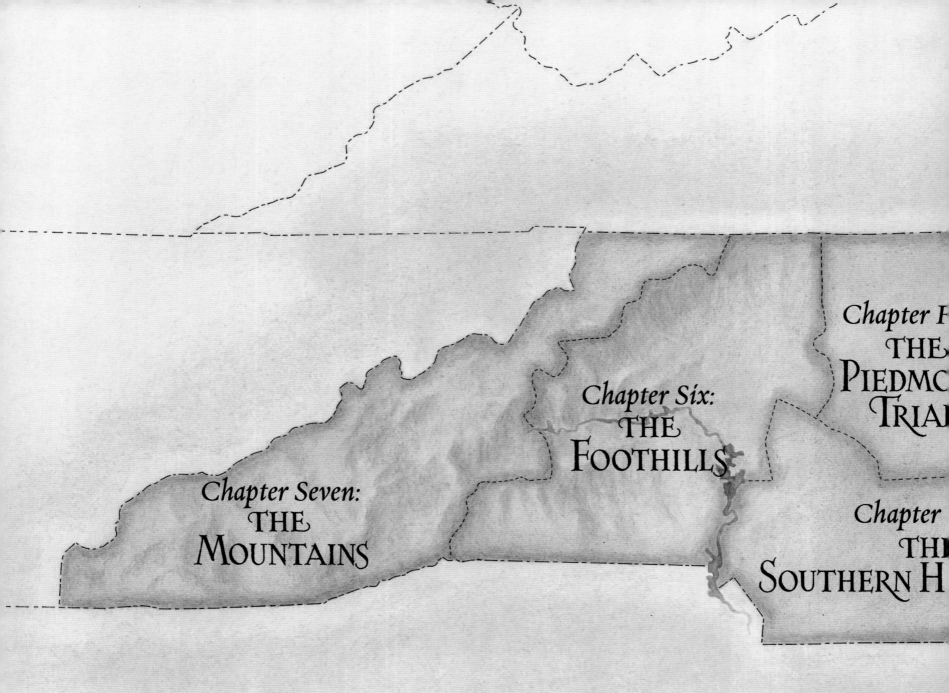

Finding Your Way:
MAP OF REGIONS

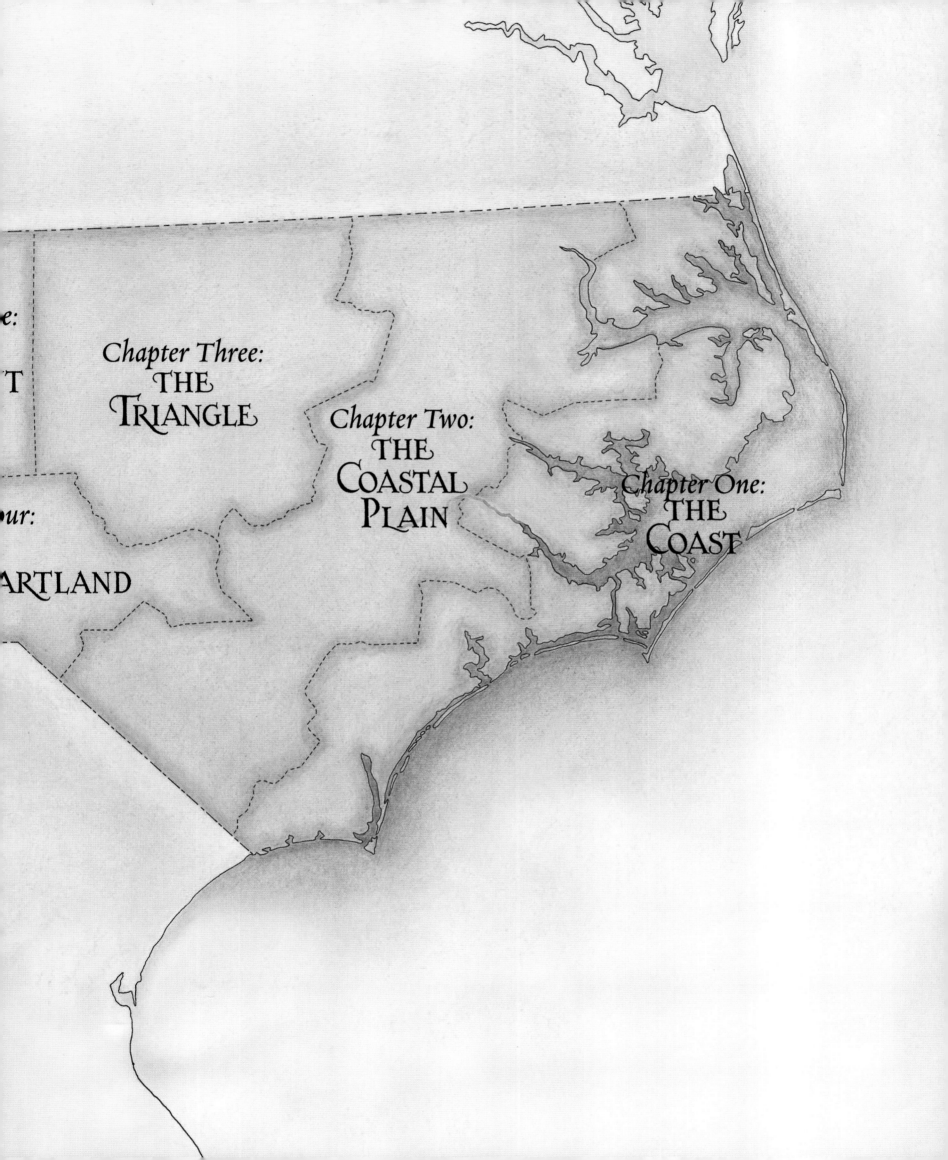

INTRODUCTION

Like many North Carolinians in the 1960s, I grew up in the church. In our home, Sunday was not a day of work or play but a day of worship, family, and rest.

The Sunday ritual actually began on Saturday afternoon when my father prepared the main dishes and desserts for our Sunday dinner — a roast or ham or chicken, as well as a pie or two. My sister and brothers and I were scrubbed clean, and my mother often spent the evening practicing the hymns she would play in church the next morning.

There was never a question about whether we were going to church. The only question was whether my mother would play for the 11 o'clock worship service in addition to playing for her Sunday school class. And, of course, for my sister, what dress to wear. She subscribed to a wonderfully bewildering set of laws governing which patent leather shoes could be worn precisely on which weekend of the year; matching gloves and dresses were subject to strict criteria. Dressing my brothers, on the other hand, resembled an exercise in herding cats. Despite the grand scale of preparation and somewhat miraculously, however, we were never late.

Mount Pisgah United Methodist Church on the outskirts of Greensboro was a classic Piedmont North Carolina brick church with a pristine white steeple. Ours was a handsome sanctuary with rich green carpet and chocolate pews where the faithful gathered for inspiration, revelation, and friendship in the orderly structure of Methodism.

I typically positioned myself between my father and mother, when she wasn't playing the piano or organ, primarily to unalign my pompous self with the mischievousness of my brothers, who at least outwardly seemed blissfully unaffected by the titanic theological questions being presented before us.

Though slight in stature, the minister always spoke with authority, precision, and kindness, and thoughtful words flowed from his baritone voice like a storyteller. I loved to hear him tell tales from the Bible, which he delivered with great theater and surprise. My favorite was when Mary went to Jesus' grave and He was gone, but I secretly wished Noah had uninvited snakes on the ark. After all, hadn't they already messed up Eden?

As I grew older, I began to struggle with the steep concepts laid out each week by the minister — big words that weren't on any of my spelling lists yet, like depravity and salvation, mortality and resurrection, nativity and epiphany. I realized

continued on page 21

continued from page 19

the enormity of them because, from the pulpit, the minister preached about our affirmations of faith and transgressions with gravity and concern, and no one chuckled like they did when he joked about beating the Baptists to the K&W Cafeteria.

These seemingly confusing and conflicting notions consumed me and I worried continually about them. What was a sin? Was I old enough to have one? Would we all go to heaven together? I wasn't sure where it was, but I knew I didn't want to go there without my mom and dad. And I already had a great dad, why would I have another one? How old would I be when I got to heaven? Would I finally get to meet my grandfathers? If the streets were lined with gold, I bet God wasn't a teacher like my parents were. We certainly didn't live on a gold-lined street. And if God was so perfect, why did giraffes have such long necks and skinny legs?

Then, during one cool Easter sunrise service when I was about 12, the haziness of the minister's sermons began to clear. We arrived at the designated time, as usual, and my mom took her seat at the piano. My siblings shuffled down the regular pew on which we sat, followed by my father and me. The service began with a joyous welcome from the minister, an overture of the morning's theme of redemption and hope. Then, we opened our hymnals to #154 and began singing "Christ the Lord Is Risen Today."

The voices of the singing congregation filled the sanctuary, transcendent in their beauty and in the rejoicing message they carried. Awakening rays of sunlight streamed through the sanctuary's wrinkled panes of glass and the early morning April chill disappeared. A slight tear trickled down my cheek and landed on my father's hand. Without pause, he leaned down and gently kissed the top of my head. Then he closed the hymnal and sang the remaining verses by heart.

North Carolina Churches: Portraits of Grace is a celebration of the memories, legends, and voices that make our churches such sacred places. This book is not intended to be a comprehensive examination of religion in our state, nor, despite first impressions, is it a ranking of churches by city, county, or denomination. All of the churches in our state deserve recognition in this volume; on the following pages you will find purely a sampling — 80 stories in all — of the way we, as North Carolinians, embrace, embody, and express the grace of Christianity in our houses of worship.

Mary

MARY BEST
EDITOR

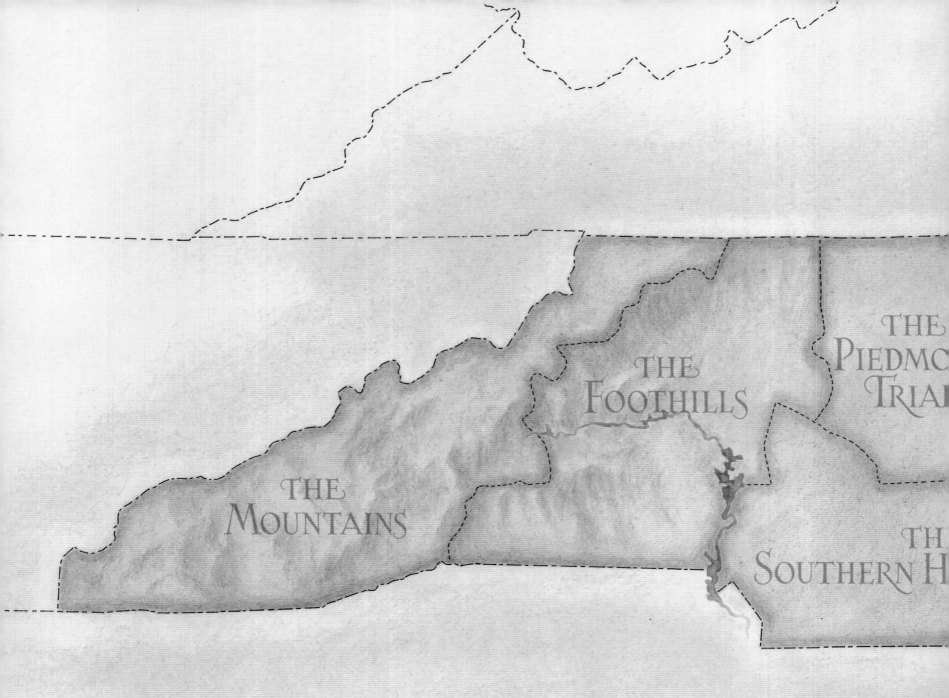

THE
PIEDMO
TRIA

THE
FOOTHILLS

THE
MOUNTAINS

THE
SOUTHERN H

CHAPTER
ONE

First, Friends

PINEY WOODS FRIENDS MEETING

Location: **Belvidere,
Perquimans County**

Current Meetinghouse
Completed: **1854**

Worship: **Regular Services**

Persecuted in England for beliefs that infuriated the mainstream churches, members of a new Protestant group known as Quakers began sailing for America in 1656 and soon found a warm reception in Perquimans County along the Albemarle Sound. Here, the Society of Friends not only established the first Quaker meeting in North Carolina, but also became the first organized religious denomination in the state, preceding even the Church of England.

Quakers trace their North Carolina beginnings to 1672, when English Friends founder George Fox and missionary William Edmundson paid separate visits to the coastal frontier and, through their preaching, triggered many conversions among colonists. The society's values of frugality and hard work, peaceful coexistence with native people, and a fundamental belief in religious freedom helped congregations flourish. In 1685 Quaker convert John Archdale became the royal governor of the two Carolinas, and soon Quakers dominated the colonial assembly.

At the peak of Quaker influence in Perquimans County, there were seven meetinghouses. Only two are left now, the oldest being Piney Woods. The venerable monthly meeting, founded in 1794, is the oldest active religious congregation in the state. Perquimans County's other active Quaker congregation, Up River Friends Meeting, was established in 1866 as an offshoot of Piney Woods. Its current church building was constructed in 1914.

The Piney Woods meetinghouse, a modest, white clapboard structure in the wooded countryside near Belvidere, dates to 1854. Its builders followed the Quaker tradition of installing a partition to create separate seating for men and women. That partition was removed in 1927 during a renovation that added a few adornments to the rather plain exterior in the form of lancet windows and a portico.

North Carolina is home today to the largest number of Quakers in the country after Indiana, despite a large exodus from the state because of their adamant opposition to slavery. As a result, the population of Friends in Perquimans County declined sharply before the Civil War, though the village of Belvidere is still predominantly Quaker. — *Mary Best*

A Prayer for Independence

ST. PAUL'S EPISCOPAL CHURCH

Location: **Edenton, Chowan County**

Church Completed: **1775**

Worship: **Regular Services**

Although Boston received more notice, Edenton was a hotbed of patriotic resistance in the years leading up to the American Revolution, and St. Paul's Episcopal Church was often found leading the cause. Weeks before the signing of the Declaration of Independence, the vestry produced a document pledging support of the Continental Congress "to the utmost of our power and ability." In August 1774, the church's rector, the Rev. Daniel Earle, led the towns-people of Edenton in a public show of support for Boston's rebellion against the Crown, declaring, "The cause of Boston is the cause of us all."

Organized under the Vestry Act of 1701, St. Paul's Parish is the oldest chartered in the state. In contrast to the neighboring colonies of Virginia and South Carolina, however, the Anglican church was weak in North Carolina — and collecting the taxes needed to build St. Paul's was difficult. Work began on the new church in 1736, but ground to a halt after 1737 with the church unfinished inside but roofed in and used for occasional services. It was not finished until 1775.

St. Paul's shady, walled churchyard includes the gravestones of three colonial governors, including town namesake Charles Eden. St. Paul's is the oldest church in the state still in active use. — *Mary Best*

"Make a Joyful Noise Unto the Lord" — *Psalm 100:1*
FIRST UNITED METHODIST CHURCH

Joyful sounds are constantly emanating from beneath the great, green dome of Elizabeth City's First United Methodist Church. That's because music-making is encouraged here — enjoyed in all its manifestations. In addition to the chancel choir, there are separate choirs for youth, pre-school-age children, and youngsters from kindergarten through fifth grade. An instrumental ensemble practices at the church on Sunday afternoons. There are also three handbell choirs — the Joy Bells, the Alleluia Ringers, and the Celebration Ringers. And then there's the church's historic (and recently regilded) pipe organ, the musical centerpiece of services held each Sunday in the sanctuary *(above)*.

The bowl shape of the dome contributes to the feeling of spaciousness in the large sanctuary and, surprisingly, it is also a source of light, as a circular stained-glass window is fixed squarely in its center. A curved balcony sweeps around the sides and back of the sanctuary in a graceful arc, bring-ing seating capacity in the church to about 650. During the late 1930s, the many seats came in handy when the church held a performance by the famous Von Trapp Family, about whom the musical *The Sound of Music* was later written.

Credit for the church's magnificent design (an architectural style called "Protestant Neoclassical") goes to Charlotte architect James McMichael, whose signature dome can be found on several prominent churches in North Carolina. The first sermon delivered under this particular dome was preached in 1922.

The church currently numbers about 715 members, many of whom live out of town but still maintain their membership for sentimental reasons. About 225 people typically attend the traditional 11 a.m. Sunday worship service, which is also broadcast by a local radio station. Recently, the church began offering an 8:30 a.m. contemporary service on Sunday as well. It's a less formal — though still musical — service, with the sounds of piano, guitar, and praise songs replacing the choir, organ, and traditional hymns. — *Kathy Grant Westbrook*

Location: **Elizabeth City, Pasquotank County**

Current Church Completed: **1922**

Worship: **Regular Services**

Moving in Mysterious Ways
PROVIDENCE UNITED METHODIST CHURCH

Many folks in the small coastal town of Swan Quarter believe that God sometimes moves in mysterious ways. They point to an old church there, the former Providence United Methodist — often referred to as "the church moved by the hand of God" — as tangible evidence.

The story begins in 1874, when local Methodists who had been worshiping in a temporary location decided to build a church of their own. A site committee found the perfect piece of land — it was in the heart of town and at its highest elevation. There was just one problem: The owner of the lot, Sam Sadler, wouldn't sell. The disappointed Methodists settled instead for a different lot, and they built a small church that rested on brick piers. They called it Methodist Episcopal Church South.

September 16, 1876, brought a storm of heavy rains and high winds, which triggered floodwaters all over Hyde County. The next morning — the day the new church was to be dedicated — the floodwaters rose higher as the tide came in, until they proved too strong for the church and carried it into what is now Oyster Creek Road. The church floated down the road to a corner — now the corner of Oyster Creek Road and U.S. Highway 264 Business — and bumped into a general store.

Then the building made a 90-degree right turn and headed down that road for a couple of blocks. At that point, it veered slightly, took another left turn, jumped over the 14-foot-wide Carawan Canal, and landed on Sam Sadler's property, the very lot that the church members had wanted all along.

A stunned — and perhaps frightened — Sam Sadler changed his mind and deeded the lot to the church. When the church was dedicated a few years later, is it any wonder they changed the name to Providence?

The story may sound a little fishy, but it has been documented. In 1939, Swan Quarter native Lelia Brinn, an eyewitness to the event, swore in an affidavit that it really happened. Since then, the story has been handed down for generations.

The little church building served as the sanctuary for Providence until 1913, when a new church was built on the property. The old church was sold for use as a barn, but in the 1940s, after the owners died, their daughters gave the building to the church as a memorial. It was renovated and used as a preschool, educational building, and fellowship hall.

In recent years, Providence has experienced more turbulent waters. In 1999, Hurricane Floyd brought extensive flooding that damaged not only the historic building, but also the newer sanctuary. After an extensive renovation, the congregation returned to its improved house of worship in September 2003. A Wednesday evening service was held there, followed by a Sunday morning service — and then Hurricane Isabel struck.

As a result of that damage — coupled with dwindling membership at Providence and other area Methodist churches — Providence merged in 2004 with nearby Soule, Bethany, Engelhard, and Amity United Methodist churches, to form Soule United Methodist Church.

Meanwhile, the old church is open to visitors and used for special events. Local leaders are pursuing a historic preservation designation for it, according to the Rev. Ken Davenport, who served as Providence's senior pastor. "There's too much history there," he added. "That building would never be demolished." — *Jimmy Tomlin*

Location: **Swan Quarter, Hyde County**

Original Church Completed: **1874**

Worship: **Old Church Building Open to Visitors; Regular Services Now Held at Soule United Methodist Church**

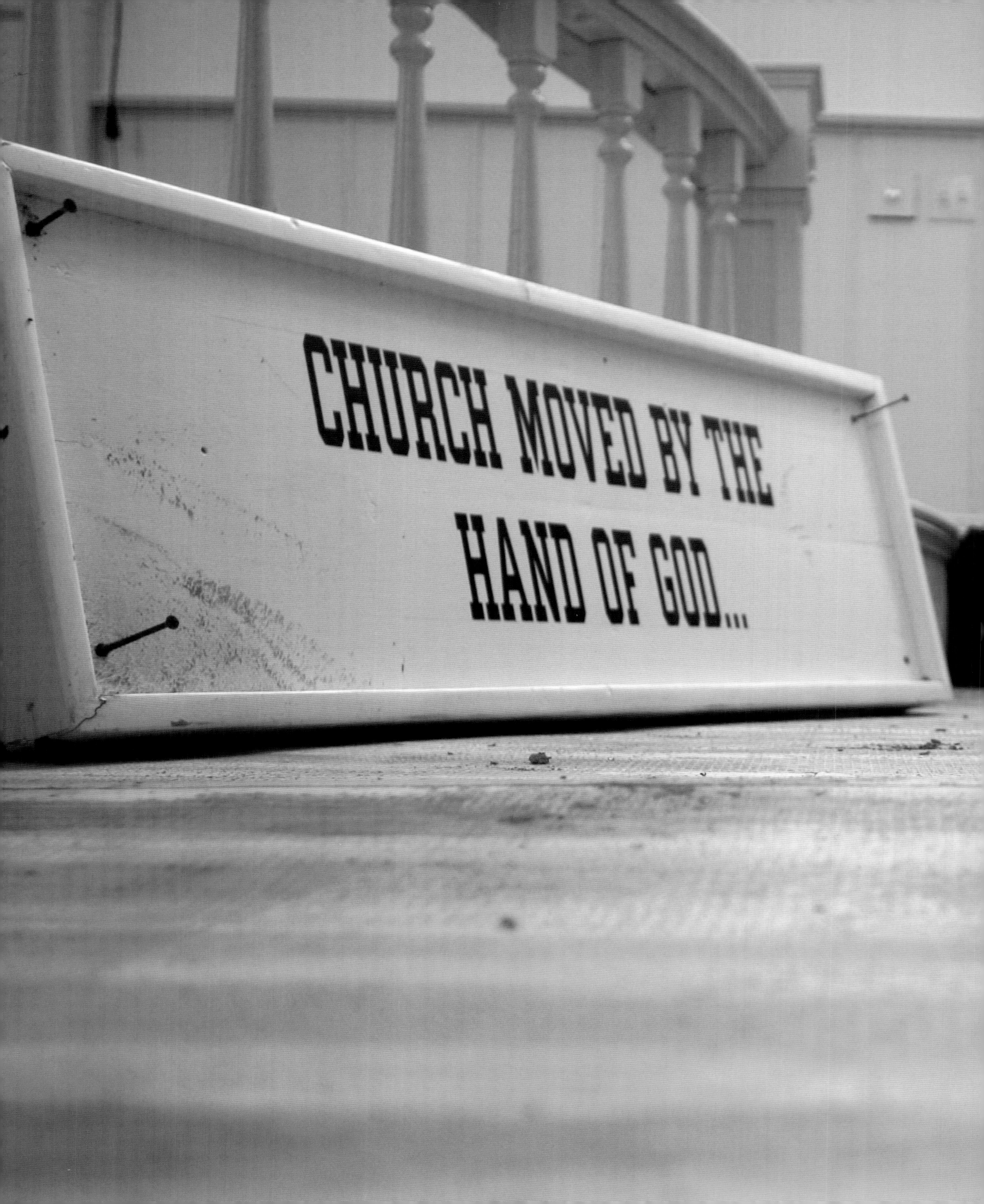
CHURCH MOVED BY THE
HAND OF GOD...

WHEN IT RAINS, IT POURS: When Hurricane Isabel struck, Providence sustained extensive damage. "We had about four feet of water in the sanctuary," the Rev. Ken Davenport said. "From the windows up, the church was fine. From the windows down, it was not so good."

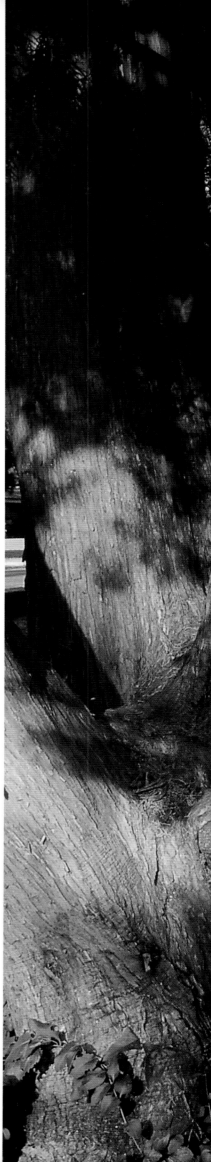

In the Beginning
ST. THOMAS EPISCOPAL CHURCH

Location: **Bath,
Beaufort County**

Church Built: **1734**

Worship: **Regular Services**

History looms large at diminutive St. Thomas Episcopal Church, the oldest church in North Carolina in the oldest town in North Carolina. European settlers first began arriving along Bath Creek on the north side of the Pamlico River in the 1690s, and by 1701 the population was large enough for the Church of England to establish St. Thomas Parish of Bath. In 1734 came construction of the church that stands today at the corner of Craven and Harding streets. Built of locally fired brick and a mortar made of crushed oyster shells, St. Thomas went up quickly.

Stained-glass windows and other Victorian features were added in the 1880s but have since been removed, returning the brick church to its simple colonial look. Although the structure does not have a spire, a small wooden bell tower, with Queen Anne's Bell, sits on the grounds. Among St. Thomas' most prized artifacts are two silver candelabras, a gift from King George II in 1740, and a communion chalice from the Bishop of London in 1747. The candlesticks and chalice are still used during High Holy Day services. Also cherished is the one remaining book from a 1,000-tome collection given to the parish in 1701 by an English missionary society. With the books, the frontier settlement established the first public library in North Carolina.

The famous "Bath Curse" — one explanation for why the thriving port never grew into the large city it seemed destined to become — originated at St. Thomas Church during the Great Awakening of the mid-1700s. According to legend, visiting evangelist George Whitefield was so unhappy with the congregation's lukewarm reaction to his fiery sermon that he put a curse on the town — saying it would forever remain a small village. — *David La Vere*

Rise and Shine
CHRIST EPISCOPAL CHURCH

Location: **New Bern, Craven County**

Current Church Completed: **1885**

Worship: **Regular Services**

Punctuated with a golden crown, the bell tower and spire of Christ Episcopal Church have risen above New Bern since the late 1800s. It is one of the seaport town's most visible landmarks, so much so that the steeple even appeared on mariners' navigational charts.

The church was Anglican at its beginnings before the American Revolution, and as such became the recipient of a congratulatory silver communion service from England's King George II. The church keeps the treasured items on display.

Christ Church's first rector, James Reed, worked hard to strengthen the church. He once described the parish he served as being at least 100 miles long with an unknown number of Anglican communicants, plus "dissenters of all denominations from New England, particularly Anabaptists, Methodists, Quakers, and Presbyterians," a few Catholics, and about 1,000 "Infidels & Heathens." When a Methodist minister passed through New Bern in 1772, however, he complimented Reed's flock as "the genteelest congregation I have seen since I left Philadelphia."

A stained-glass window above the altar memorializes a later chapter in the church's history, when the congregation struggled to rebuild after the Civil War. It depicts Jesus' blessing of the children and was made possible through the money young girls of the parish made from selling their homemade handicrafts. — *Mary Best*

"Hearing the Word of God Fully Preached"
FIRST PRESBYTERIAN CHURCH

Location: **New Bern,
Craven County**

Current Church Completed:
1822

Worship: **Regular Services**

If it weren't for Catherine Green Stanly and her diary, not much would be known today about the early years of First Presbyterian Church. Her book survived the fire that destroyed the church's official records before 1827.

In her own right, Stanly was one of the most memorable members of the little group of 10 women and three men who founded the church in 1817. Born a slave, she was freed by her husband, John, who rose from slavery himself to become one of New Bern's wealthiest men.

The congregation at first worshiped in a Baptist meetinghouse, but with the support of a number of leading businessmen they soon began drawing plans for a church of their own. The cornerstone was laid in 1819 for the graceful and audaciously large building — capable of seating 800. In her diary entry for January 6, 1822, Catherine Stanly wrote: "Sabbath evening: To-day the Presbyterian Church was dedicated to the worship of God. ... I have been blessed with the privilege of hearing the Word of God faithfully preached."

During the Civil War, regular services stopped at First Presbyterian and the church and its grounds were used by Union troops as a hospital. The belfry still bears the names and initials that the occupying soldiers carved into the wood. — *Mary Best*

Safe Harbor

ANN STREET UNITED METHODIST CHURCH

Location: **Beaufort, Carteret County**

Church Built: **1854**

Worship: **Regular Services**

At one with Beaufort's maritime heritage, Ann Street United Methodist Church possesses an elegant coastal simplicity of white-painted planks and cedar siding, capped by a steeple that once served to guide ships into Beaufort Harbor.

Inside, nautical themes symbolize a spiritually independent people at home with their God on the edge of the sea. Shipbuilders who helped in its construction gave the wooden ceiling the strength of a ship's hull by placing boards at cross-angles, and it has stood the test of time and storm.

Ann Street Methodist marks 1778 as the date it was founded; it was the year members began using an abandoned Anglican church building for services when the revival spirit of Methodism swept through the town. Growing slowly but steadily, the congregation in 1820 built a larger church, Purvis Chapel, half a block away. Growing still, they completed the current church at the corner of Ann and Craven streets in 1854 and donated their old chapel to the A.M.E. Zion Church, which still uses it today.

Union troops during the Civil War turned the church into a hospital and troops bivouacked in the parsonage. Reclaiming the church after the war, the congregation began a series of enhancements, including installation of its many stained-glass windows *(right)*. An extraordinary story is attached to a window created to honor 19th-century congregation members Robert and Mary Chadwick. According to church history, the couple befriended and helped educate a Chinese lad who arrived in the United States as a ship's stowaway. The boy, Charles Soong, later returned to his homeland, where he reared a highly distinguished family. One daughter became Madame Chiang Kai-shek, legendary wife of the leader of Taiwan. Another daughter married Sun Yat-sen, considered the "father of modern China."

Dating from the early 1700s, the Old Burying Ground adjacent to the church is filled with weathered tombstones and vaults *(above)*. It is the final resting place of an 18th-century British Navy officer whose request to be buried standing upright, facing England, was honored. Captain Otway Burns, an American naval hero of the War of 1812, is also entombed here, his grave topped by a cannon from his ship, the *Snap Dragon*. — *David La Vere*

Sing a Song of Gladness
ST. JAMES EPISCOPAL CHURCH

Welcoming worshipers since 1840, St. James Episcopal is the oldest existing church building in Wilmington. The Gothic Revival landmark is home to a congregation that dates much farther back, established in 1729 by the Church of England.

Construction of their first church began in 1751 and was completed in 1770. Too soon, the American Revolution brought the war to its door. During Lord Cornwallis' occupation of Wilmington in 1781, his troops turned St. James into a stable and riding academy. The church survived the occupation, however, and was returned to the congregation after the war.

As the church thrived in the 1800s, plans were drawn for a larger, more architecturally spectacular church. The old church was torn down and its bricks used in the new construction half a block away. That saved money, as did the decision not to erect a spire but use a tower decorated with battlements instead *(right)*.

One of St. James' most cherished possessions is an oil painting of Christ titled *Ecce Homo* ("Behold the Man"), believed to be the work of 17th-century Spanish artist Francisco Pacheco. It was salvaged by colonists from the ruins of a Spanish ship that exploded on the Cape Fear River in 1748. The painting, which hangs in the sanctuary, depicts Christ wrapped in a red cloak and wearing a crown of thorns during His trial before Pontius Pilate.

Like many Wilmington churches, St. James faced difficult times during the Civil War. During Union occupation, the pews were thrown outside and the sanctuary was used as a hospital. The Rev. Alfred Watson incensed Union officers by praying for the health of Confederate President Jefferson Davis and refusing to do the same for Abraham Lincoln. They retaliated by abolishing services there.

In the aftermath of the war and a yellow fever epidemic in 1862, morale was low in Wilmington, and Watson pondered how to lift his congregation's spirits. On Easter morning 1866, he led the St. James children's choir up several flights of stairs *(above)* to the church tower, and at sunrise they began to sing. Their songs carried out across the town, and people gathered around the church to rejoice in their first Easter since the war's end. The tradition continues to this day, expanded now to welcome all who wish to join in the chorus. — *David La Vere*

Location: **Wilmington, New Hanover County**

Current Church Completed: **1840**

Worship: **Regular Services**

"A Great Cathedral at Wilmington"
FIRST BAPTIST CHURCH

Location: **Wilmington, New Hanover County**

Church Completed: **1870**

Worship: **Regular Services**

John Lamb Prichard envisioned First Baptist Church as "a great cathedral at Wilmington," large enough for 1,000 parishioners, and it turned out every bit as beautiful as the pastor had dreamed. The church's story is one of joy and triumph. But it is also one of profound sadness along the way.

Construction of the grand church got under way in 1860, but was interrupted within a year by the outbreak of the Civil War. In 1862, yellow fever swept the city, and among its victims was Prichard, who had sent his family away to safety but insisted on staying behind to give comfort to his congregation.

In January 1865 Wilmington residents climbed to the top of the unfinished First Baptist Church to watch Union forces win the Battle of Fort Fisher 20 miles away. The end of the war was not far off, and with it came resumption of work on the church. And, in 1870, amid much rejoicing, it was done.

The church is a vision of cherry-stained heart pine and stained glass; the pews hand-carved and numbered. (At one time, parishioners paid rent on them to help pay for the church's construction.) Underneath it all, the church stands like a rock — its foundation built from ballast stones discarded by sailing ships as they took on cargo at Wilmington's docks.

The winds of Hurricane Fran in 1996 collapsed one of the church's tall spires and sent bricks and timber crashing onto Market Street below. But the spire was rebuilt, made stronger with metal interior beams, and the tower's original slate roof also was restored. The church's one-ton bell still peals every Sunday morning, calling the faithful to worship.

The Rev. John Lamb Prichard would be proud. — *David La Vere*

LUOLA'S CHAPEL
ERECTED TO THE
GLORY AND WORSHIP
OF GOD

BY LUOLA
BELOVED WIFE
OF JAMES SPRUNT
1915

No Greater Love
LUOLA'S CHAPEL

Nestled amid the showcase gardens of Orton Plantation, the picturesque little church known as Luola's Chapel was built for family services at a time when the nearest house of worship was miles away. The chapel is named for the beloved lady of the estate, Luola Sprunt, who died while it was being built. Fittingly, this memorial to love is today a popular setting for weddings.

The classic antebellum estate has been owned by the same family since 1884, when former Civil War colonel Kenneth McKenzie Murchison bought and began restoring the deserted rice plantation. At his death in 1904, the property went to his daughter Luola and son-in-law James Sprunt. Under Luola's guidance, Orton began to bloom. In 1910, she directed that wings be added to the plantation house. She personally planted many of the trees around the grounds and also developed its first flower gardens. Today, there are more than 20 acres of lawns, gardens, walking paths, and waterways.

In 1915, construction of the family chapel got under way. "Roads were bad back then, and that made it difficult for people to go to church," Kenneth Sprunt, a direct descendent, said. "And my grandfather was a devout Presbyterian." Luola died in 1916 before the chapel was finished, but her memory lives on here. A painted glass window *(left)* in the chancel wall bears the inscription: "Luola's Chapel. Erected to the Glory and Worship of God. By Luola. Beloved Wife of James Sprunt."

After Luola's death, James stayed at the plantation only in winter and spring, and services at the chapel were sporadic. The philanthropist and author died in 1924.

To keep it in harmony with the plantation house, Luola's Chapel was designed in the Greek Revival style. The chapel remains a quiet, meditative place, painted a soft, robin's egg blue and laid out in the shape of a cross. The pews are original and still have doors at the aisle to keep out cold winter drafts that creep up from the Cape Fear River.

The 9,000-acre Orton Plantation remains a private residence, but its magnificent gardens are open to the public and Luola's Chapel is available for wedding ceremonies. — *David La Vere*

Location: **Orton Plantation, Winnabow, Brunswick County**

Chapel Completed: **1916**

Worship: **Open for Weddings and Visitation March Through November (except Thanksgiving Day)**

PARADISE FOUND: Facing the mighty Cape Fear River, Luola's Chapel sits amid its namesake's Eden-like gardens and only a few hundred yards from the plantation house.

This Little Light of Mine
VILLAGE CHAPEL

Location: **Bald Head Island, Brunswick County**

Church Completed: **1987**

Worship: **Regular Services**

Built in the shadow of the oldest standing lighthouse in North Carolina, the Village Chapel on Bald Head Island has been welcoming residents and visitors of all faiths since 1987. Filled to capacity for Sunday services when summer tourists crowd the island, the little church is open 24 hours a day.

Bald Head, a privately owned resort development accessible by ferry from Southport, lacked enough year-round homeowners until the mid-1980s to organize a church service. Led by a Presbyterian minister, residents, developers, and guests came together at the Bald Head Inn on Easter Sunday in 1984 for the first worship service to take place on the island in modern times. Informal Sunday services continued after that while plans took shape to build a church.

The Mitchell family, developers of the island, donated land for the project. Homeowners obtained a $90,000 construction loan and paid it off by holding barbecues, bake sales, quilt raffles, and art shows, and even more creatively, by selling medallions inscribed with donors' names. The golden medallions are inlaid in the altar rail.

Residents also worked out the design. The painted cedar exterior and short steeple reflect architecture common in 19th-century coastal Carolina. Because the site is next to the 1817 Old Baldy Lighthouse and overlooks Bald Head Creek, clear glass windows were placed behind the pulpit and exposed beams were used to accentuate the sense of oneness with nature. Above the back gallery, a stained-glass window depicts three fishes in an equilateral triangle, a subtle mingling of Christian and coastal motifs.

The Village Chapel is ecumenical and has no full-time pastor. Instead, there is a different guest minister each Sunday — and interest is so great among visiting clergy that the chapel is booked a year in advance.

Easter Sunrise services are particularly special, with the pastor delivering the sermon from the steps of Old Baldy Lighthouse. — *David La Vere*

THE
PIEDMO
TRIA

THE
FOOTHILLS

THE
MOUNTAINS

THE
SOUTHERN H

CHAPTER
TWO

THE
TRIANGLE

THE
COASTAL
PLAIN

THE
COAST

ARTLAND

Faith of Our Fathers
PHILADELPHUS PRESBYTERIAN CHURCH

Organized by Scottish immigrants who brought their Presbyterian beliefs, Highland traditions, and Gaelic language to North Carolina in the 1700s, Philadelphus Church's history and heritage are kept alive today by a small but faithful congregation.

Before the building of their first church, worshipers met in private homes and were led by itinerant ministers who conducted services in both Gaelic and English. In 1799, they held their first communion in a tent built specially for the occasion. They moved into their first church building about 1802 and eventually outgrew it. The large Greek Revival church that stands today was begun in 1859 and dedicated in 1861.

Dominated by two 16-sided Doric columns at the front entrance, the white wooden church stands out in its country setting *(right)*. Green plantation shutters cover its many windows. The belfry tower, topped by a pyramidal roof, holds the church's original bell.

There are four entrances. Presbyterians in the mid-19th century believed that genders and races should be segregated at worship. White men and white women entered the sanctuary through separate doors and sat on opposite sides of a wooden divider that ran down the middle pews. Two other entrances, for black men and black women, led up spiral wooden staircases to side and back galleries overlooking the sanctuary.

In 1961, the church's 100th anniversary, the interior was treated to a major refurbishment. The church was entered on the National Register of Historic Places in 1975.

A carefully maintained cemetery behind the church contains several hundred graves, the oldest dating to 1863. The names on grave markers underscore the church's Highland Scot heritage.

Philadelphus Presbyterian Church has not had a permanent minister since 1939, when the Rev. Neil McInnis died. Since then, the flock has relied on part-time and visiting ministers, including clergy from St. Andrews Presbyterian College in Laurinburg, to lead Sunday services. Though worshipers are few now, typically numbering about 30 each Sunday, many more of the faithful return on the first Sunday in November for homecoming services.

As the church history points out, these "strong and faithful" members continue "sharing the faith and maintaining God's church," a tradition begun many generations ago by their Highland Scot ancestors. — *David La Vere*

Location: **Red Springs, Robeson County**

Current Church Completed: **1861**

Worship: **Regular Services**

Going Home
PROSPECT UNITED METHODIST CHURCH

Prospect United Methodist Church illustrates the concept of outreach in the most basic and exemplary way — bringing families together in joy and solace and caring for those in need. It is, in a real sense, the heart of this old and tightly knit Indian community.

The church at the end of Onnie-Joe Road five miles west of Pembroke traces its beginnings as far back as 1865. Some of the founding members of the church were relatives of Henry Berry Lowrie, the cultural hero of Native American people from Robeson County.

Early on, Prospect Church served as a school for area children. Today, as one of the largest Native American churches in the county, the 987 members concentrate on making sure needy families have food on the table and support through any number of life's challenges. The church distributes 25,000 pounds of food each year. In addition, it sponsors a plate dinner sale and charity golf tournament to raise funds for people in need of emergency money. More than $20,000 each year goes to help individuals and families with heating and electric bills and medical emergencies, as well as to enable loved ones to be near family members who have extended hospital stays.

The caring and togetherness of this community were illustrated in traditional fashion on November 29, 2003, when a crowd gathered at the church to celebrate the wedding of the minister's daughter, Allison Locklear, to Derek Lowry *(right)*. It was also the celebration of a homecoming. After 18 years in Greensboro, where he headed the Indian education program for the school system, Derek realized his dream of returning to his family and the Tuscarora people. In enormous sadness, tragically, the community came together at the church a little more than a month later to mourn his untimely passing. This outstanding native son suffered a fatal heart attack on New Year's Day. — *Mark Wagoner*

Author's Note: Derek Lowry and I became close friends during his years in Greensboro, and I was delighted to attend his wedding to Allison at Prospect Church. January 4, 2004, found me back at the church for a celebration, but this time it was for a life well lived. And it proved to be one of the saddest days of my life. I had the honor and duty of serving as a pallbearer in the funeral of my longtime friend, Derek.

Location: **Prospect, Robeson County**

Current Church Completed: **1987**

Worship: **Regular Services**

With Diligent Hands and Sturdy Faith
GROVE PRESBYTERIAN CHURCH

Location: **Kenansville, Duplin County**

Current Church Completed: **1855**

Worship: **Regular Services**

Founded by industrious and devout Scots-Irish settlers in 1736, Grove Presbyterian Church is one of the denomination's oldest congregations in North Carolina. The backcountry immigrants made their way to the area when London merchant Henry McCullough gave about 400 Scots-Irish 100 acres each to settle in southeastern North Carolina. The church takes its name from the community of Golden Grove, which later became Kenansville in Duplin County.

Even before gaining its first pastor, the self-reliant congregation built a small wooden church to hold its religious meetings. That building was burned during the American Revolution, victim of the guerrilla wars that raged between the Royalist Highland Scots settlers and the Patriot Scots-Irish. After several moves, the church built its permanent home on Main Street in 1855.

Grove Presbyterian's façade reflects the popularity of Greek Revival architecture at the time it was built, though moderated by the constraints of the rural church's finances. In 1900, triangle points were added to the originally rectangular windows to provide a Gothic Revival look.

Though updated with modern amenities, the interior of Grove Presbyterian remains a very traditional antebellum church. At the rear of the sanctuary is an upstairs gallery, originally set aside for black members. Four sets of frosted windows at the sides are fitted on the inside with wooden shutters. They were closed in the summer to keep the sanctuary cool.

Plaques in the sanctuary honor two of Grove Presbyterian's pastors, Hugh McAden and James M. Sprunt. McAden, the first Presbyterian missionary to settle in North Carolina, served the Grove congregation from 1756 to 1768. Sprunt, Grove's pastor when the Civil War broke out, left to serve as a chaplain in the Confederate Army. At war's end, he returned to the church and also served as recorder of deeds for Duplin County until his death in 1884.

The church's history room has on display the long, feather-tipped cane poles *(above)* that were used in the old days to chasten sleepy worshipers during the traditionally long Presbyterian services. Church officers patrolled the pews with the poles, waking up nappers by running the feather across their nose or ears. — *David La Vere*

F 4
GROVE CHURCH

PRESBYTERIAN. FIRST
CHURCH FOUNDED BY
SCOTCH-IRISH WHO SET-
TLED HERE ABOUT 1736.

STATE HISTORICAL COMMISSION 1936

Fit for a Queen
QUEEN STREET UNITED METHODIST CHURCH

Location: **Kinston, Lenoir County**

Current Church Completed: **1911**

Worship: **Regular Services**

Rising along one of eastern North Carolina's loveliest main streets, Queen Street United Methodist is one of downtown Kinston's crown jewels. It's called the wedding church, and it isn't difficult to understand why. The grandiose brick bastion's stained-glass windows and domed towers have captivated so many betrothed couples, both within and outside the church family, Queen Street has had to put a limit on the number of weddings it can accommodate. "Young people would drive by and see the church and decide this is the place they wanted to get married," explained church employee Teresa Smith.

But Queen Street's beauty is more than brick deep. In 1996, after the devastation of Hurricane Fran, the church answered a call for help from its community by becoming a distribution center for those in need and sent out teams to repair homes and farms.

Francis Daniel, who had been minister of the church for only three months when the storm struck, said it was during this time that he learned his congregation was a community of faith. "We have a strong linkage to the past and a strong sense of tradition," the pastor said, "but we have survived because the members continue to stay open and progressive." — *Diane Silcox-Jarrett*

Missions of Mercy
FIRST PRESBYTERIAN CHURCH

Location: **Goldsboro, Wayne County**

Current Church Completed: **1950s**

Worship: **Regular Services**

At mission-oriented First Presbyterian Church, there's always something going on. In fact, "going" is one of the things this congregation does best. Since 1995, church groups have made two mission trips to Kenya and four to Belize. The Belize team included an optometrist and a dentist who set up offices in opposite ends of a trailer and provided eyeglasses and dental care to those in need. An orthopedic surgeon made the trip to Kenya, performing the first knee-replacement operation in that country and teaching the procedure to local doctors.

Recognizing the needs of those closer to home, church members have journeyed to West Virginia four times and made several outings in North Carolina to help with post-hurricane cleanup and rebuilding. Youth in the church have followed the example set by the adults, carrying out numerous mission trips of their own. One of the church's greatest accomplishments can be found in Goldsboro itself, the building of a retirement village for senior citizens.

First Presbyterian's own home is a 25,000-square-foot brick structure on Ash Street. At the opposite end of the scale, size-wise, is the congregation's original building *(above)*, also on Ash Street, built in 1856 and consisting of just a sanctuary and storage room. After the congregation moved in the 1950s, the building served for a number of years as a meeting hall for the Wayne County Historical Association. It is now a church again, leased to the Spirit-Filled Family Worship Center. — *Kathy Grant Westbrook*

"Thou Shalt Come into the Ark" — *Genesis 6:18*
EUREKA UNITED METHODIST CHURCH

Location: **Eureka, Wayne County**

Current Church Completed: **1884**

Worship: **Regular Services**

Farms line the country road in northern Wayne County that leads to Eureka United Methodist Church. The quiet, rural highway winds past one white clapboard farmhouse after another before reaching the cross-roads of Eureka. Just past a row of turn-of-the-century storefronts stands the spotless white frame church. Built in 1884, Eureka United Methodist Church has served as not only a house of worship but also the social and cultural center of this farming community for more than a century. With Gothic Revival touches, the inviting exterior resembles many fine churches that dot the eastern North Carolina landscape with its weatherboard frame, lancet windows filled with wavy glass, central entrance, belfry, and gabled roof.

But the most distinguishing feature of Eureka United Methodist Church adorns the inside. Above the sanctuary stretches an intricately shaped wooden ceiling, skillfully crafted of Carolina yellow pine to form the shape of an ark.

The shelter of Eureka's ark has reached beyond this intimate community of about 300. The memory of its spiritual strength and warmth helped Stanley Yelverton survive in a German prisoner-of-war camp while serving in the U.S. Army during World War II. "When I was in the POW camp thoughts about my church brought me comfort," he remembered. "We had one Bible between us in the camp and when we would pass it around I would think about hearing God's word on Sunday mornings back in Eureka." Sunday morning memories were not the only ones Yelverton had. "I would think about those Sunday picnics, too. We had some good food — fried chicken, cherry pie, and cakes," he laughed. Through those long days Yelverton felt the members of Eureka were praying for him. "I could feel the prayers coming my way. I knew the people cared for me." — *Diane Silcox-Jarrett*

Amazing Grace
BEAR GRASS PRIMITIVE BAPTIST CHURCH

On the third Sunday of each month, visitors listening outside Bear Grass Primitive Baptist Church will hear more than a dozen voices singing age-old hymns in natural harmony. No organ or piano accompanies them — just the tradition of music as beloved melodies waft over the Martin County countryside.

About 20 people attend the monthly worship service at Bear Grass. They arrive about 10:30 and spend the first half hour singing from a hymnbook that has no notes, only words. People take turns calling out the names of hymns they want to sing. "Amazing Grace" is a favorite; it is sung pretty much every Sunday. Listen long enough and you're likely to hear "Rock of Ages" or "How Firm a Foundation." Through the course of 30 minutes, the voices never waver.

After the singing comes the preaching. Elder Harold Pittman has been delivering sermons at Bear Grass for about 12 years. Church member Vader Hodges said, "We have a real good preacher. He can get up there and talk for 30 minutes and never take a breath."

Hodges, 71, has attended Bear Grass her entire life, although she didn't become a member until 1993. Her roots in the church run deep: Her great-grandfather preached here, as did her grandfather, B.S. Cowin. "When I was growing up, the church would be full," Hodges recalled.

Although the number of members has declined in recent years, Bear Grass doesn't rely on numbers to find meaning. Constancy and faithful adherence to the Scriptures are basic tenets of the Primitive Baptist theology. For decades, Sunday services have been conducted in the same order and manner, although men and women no longer enter through the building's separate entrances and sit on separate sides of the sanctuary. The church's stark interior has undergone a few changes, for the comfort and convenience of the congregation. Restrooms were added about 50 years ago, and gas heaters replaced two wood stoves just recently.

In keeping with the strict biblical interpretations of Primitive Baptists, there is foot washing at Bear Grass once a year. "Men wash men's feet and women wash women's feet," explained Hodges. Afghans are draped across the slat-backed bench pews to provide the women with privacy where they gather.

Like many other Primitive Baptist churches, Bear Grass is beautiful in its simplicity. Built in 1829, the white meetinghouse has maintained its unadorned exterior. The sanctuary is wrapped in yellow pine, its walls and ceiling covered with this richly colored wood. Homemade cushions and afghans of varying colors and designs are placed on a few of the pews, separated by two aisles, near the front of the church. Large windows line the walls, inviting light to pour in and allowing the melody of "Amazing Grace" to slip out. — *Kathy Grant Westbrook*

Location: **Bear Grass, Martin County**

Church Completed: **1829**

Worship: **Services Held the Third Sunday of the Month**

"IN REMEMBRANCE OF ME:" Four times a year, Bear Grass holds communion, led by Elder Harold Pittman (*right*). With the help of Vader Hodges (*top left*), a hardy church dinner follows each communion service. Makeshift tables for holding the food are fashioned from large pieces of plywood spread across pews. The other Sundays during the year when Bear Grass holds services, Hodges cooks dinner at her own home for anyone from the church who wishes to join her.

Grace Under Pressure
GRACE EPISCOPAL CHURCH

Grace Episcopal Church was not spared when the little town of Plymouth became a major battle zone during the Civil War, owing to its strategic location on the Roanoke River. The church's brand-new pews were chopped up for firewood and pieced together for coffins. The sanctuary was used to house soldiers' horses and goats.

But at war's end, battered Grace Episcopal found sympathy and kindness in its hour of need. A Union Army chaplain, sizing up the damage to the church, headed a campaign to raise money for repairs. Thanks to his efforts, the altar, pulpit, windows, and pews were replaced, and the church was once again open for worship.

Another Civil War story associated with the church — and one that admittedly belongs in the category of local legend — tells of a peddler who amassed a small fortune selling provisions to Union troops. Worried that he might be robbed, so the story goes, he stole away to Grace Episcopal during the night and buried his money in the churchyard. The truth of the story has never been proved one way or the other — though there have been at least two nighttime visitors who tried their luck at finding the buried treasure and left empty-handed.

Members say it isn't uncommon for visitors passing through Plymouth to stop by Grace Episcopal, hoping to get a peek inside or to stroll through the old cemetery with its view of the swiftly flowing Roanoke River. No doubt, if any visitor has heard the story of the church's sycamore trees, they will also be looking for them.

The story, a favorite among members, goes like this: Twelve sycamore trees were planted in the churchyard in the 19th century, and each was given the name of an apostle of Christ. During a violent thunderstorm, the tree named Judas was hit by lightning and killed. The others were spared. Unfortunately, none of the famous trees remain today, having been lost to disease or damage over the years. — *Kathy Grant Westbrook*

Location: **Plymouth, Washington County**

Current Church Completed: **1861**

Worship: **Regular Services**

Heaven and Nature Sing
CALVARY EPISCOPAL CHURCH

The churchyard at Calvary Episcopal Church was once described as so beautiful — it could be dangerous to a person's health. According to a favorite local story, the Rev. Joseph Blount Cheshire was working in the garden one day when an old-timer stopped by to warn him that he was "making this yard so pretty," he was "'ticing folks to die."

That was in the 19th century, and today the rector's sophisticated landscaping arrangement of trees, shrubs, and winding paths amid the grave markers is more than ever regarded as one of North Carolina's most enticing urban garden spots.

Cheshire had arrived in the area in the 1840s as a young priest to serve a church in Scotland Neck. But when the senior warden of Calvary invited him to come visit and preach, he agreed to take charge of the Tarboro congregation as well. The avid gardener soon had the churchyard fenced in and began to transform it into a thing of rare beauty. Generations of gardeners have since maintained and enhanced his beloved garden, with the maturing trees shading gravestones of every era.

The garden was taking shape as the vestry began drawing plans to replace its old frame church with the brick house of worship that stands today, a classic Gothic Revival designed by architect William Percival with towers, spires, buttresses, and pointed arches. Construction began in 1860 but was halted by the Civil War. The church was finally dedicated in 1868.

Hurricane Floyd proved in 1999 that the beauty and strength of Calvary are reflected not only in its handsome façade and grounds but also its members. With the Tar River quickly rising from the 15 inches of rain dumped on northeastern North Carolina, a young couple decided that their wedding, planned for the next day, could not wait. The bride and groom waded barefoot through the flooded churchyard and the rector arrived at the candlelit church in his hunting boots. When the rector asked, "Who gives this woman in marriage?" he held up a cell phone and the bride's father across the river shouted, "I do!"

As the church bells pealed and the party left the church, the bride placed her bouquet upon an old gravestone that still stood above water. — *Mary Best*

Location: **Tarboro, Edgecombe County**

Current Church Completed: **1868**

Worship: **Regular Services**

"O all ye Green Things upon the earth,
    bless ye the Lord ...
O ye Seas and Floods,
    bless ye the Lord."

— MORNING PRAYER,
THE BOOK OF COMMON PRAYER, 1662

Onward Christian Soldiers
REPUBLICAN BAPTIST CHURCH

A plaque in the sanctuary of Republican Baptist Church bears witness to what some folks in Bertie County refer to as a modern-day miracle.

It actually happened during the 1940s, when the United States entered into the fray of World War II. Young men and women from throughout the country were being called to military service, and those who were members of Republican Baptist were no exception. The congregation watched — and prayed — as, one by one, 36 young men and women from the church got the call to serve their country. Amazingly, all 36 returned home safely from overseas. The men's and women's names appear on the plaque *(right)*, representing a small token of thanks from a congregation filled with gratitude.

Of course, the notion of survival is nothing new to Republican Baptist, which in 2003 celebrated its 200th anniversary. According to church history, the congregation was established in 1803, and the church was officially constituted in 1834. Blessed with significant growth, in 1865 Republican Baptist had 285 members. Today, it has about 60.

Throughout its long history, Republican Baptist has tried to stay true to tradition whenever possible. One tradition that has survived — although not entirely by the church's design — is that of outdoor baptisms, a ritual that can be traced to New Testament days in the River Jordan. Few churches in North Carolina still baptize converts outdoors, as most of them now have baptismal pools or fonts in their sanctuaries.

"Republican used to have a baptismal pool in our sanctuary, but it began to leak, so they had to quit using it," said the Rev. Harvey Jackson, pastor of the church since 1985. "They would fill it up, and it would be half-empty by the time the service started." Today, new believers are baptized in a nearby farm pond, and such baptism services continue to make for special times in the spiritual life of the church.

The congregation also prides itself as a promoter of family and fellowship. "Republican has always referred to itself as a family of families, and we try to maintain that," Jackson said. "We also like to say that we'll eat at the drop of a hat — and somebody's designated to bring the hat." — *Jimmy Tomlin*

Location: **Republican, Bertie County**

Current Church Completed: **1912**

Worship: **Regular Services**

PROUDLY WE HONOR THE MEMBERS
OF OUR CHURCH WHO ANSWERED
THE CALL TO THE COLORS
RUDOLPH HOGGARD
GEO WILSON JERNIGAN
FRANCIS S. BAZEMORE
DALMUS U. BAZEMORE
LLOYD PRITCHARD
HERMAN T. HARDEN, Jr.
JOHN W. WHITE
LITTLETON BAZEMORE
HENRY B. SPRUILL
LENSIE E. WHITE
T. GILBERT BARBER
R. EARL DEMPSEY
JAS MONROE LEARY
ARCHIE WARD, Jr.
CLYDE H. DAWSON
LEWIS HENRY WEBB
ELMO J. BUTLER
THOMAS S. SPEIGHT
RALPH RAWLES
ELMAR L. LEWIS
JAMES K. BUTLER, Jr.
GEO. WORLEY WHITE
BASIL E. HARDEN
Mrs. LENA BYNUM
HAYLORD NEWSOME
J. P. HOGGARD
JOHN M. THOMAS
DONALD R. JERNIGAN
THOMAS E. COWAN
VIRGIL W. HOGGARD
HERMAN B. HUGHES
WHIT H. JERNIGAN
JESSIE C. MIZELL
LUTHER M. COWAND
JESSIE W. HARRELL

Living Happily Ever After
CHURCH OF THE IMMACULATE CONCEPTION

O nce upon a time, in the small town of Halifax, there thrived the Church of the Immaculate Conception, brimming with gingerbread tans, white trim, and spiritual enrichment. Today, although it no longer holds regular Mass, the slender, frame Catholic church continues to evoke fairy-tale beauty, spirit, and allure.

Size accounts for much of its storybook appeal; after all, any church with only 10 pews is bound to have a certain charm. Its picturesque quality can also be attributed to its late Gothic Revival style. Emphasis on vertical elements includes a steeply pitched roof and two unequal towers; the larger one has an open belfry that houses the original church bell, while the smaller one surrounds a relic chimney — a reminder of the old woodstove that once stood in the corner.

The daughters of Michael Ferrall donated funds to build the church, which was dedicated in 1889. Ferrall, a devout Catholic from Ireland, had died in 1862 after establishing himself as a successful merchant in Halifax. His family, along with that of fellow Irish immigrant Edward Conigland, are closely associated with the birth of Catholicism in Halifax.

After thriving for more than 20 years, the Church of the Immaculate Conception eventually saw its parish community dwindle to just a few. When services ceased to be held, except on an occasional basis, Ferrall's great-granddaughter Nannie Gary saw to it that the building continued to be lovingly maintained. She was the last of Ferrall's family to reside in Halifax, and, upon her death in 1969, she provided for permanent upkeep of the church in her will. Today, that responsibility falls to St. John the Baptist Parish in Roanoke Rapids.

The Church of the Immaculate Conception is the only 19th-century Gothic Revival–style frame Catholic church in North Carolina to retain so many original features and furnishings. It is also the state's only existing Catholic church known to have been designed by noted Philadelphia architect Edward F. Durang. — *Kathy Grant Westbrook*

Location: **Halifax, Halifax County**

Church Completed: **1889**

Worship: **Open Houses Held in April and December**

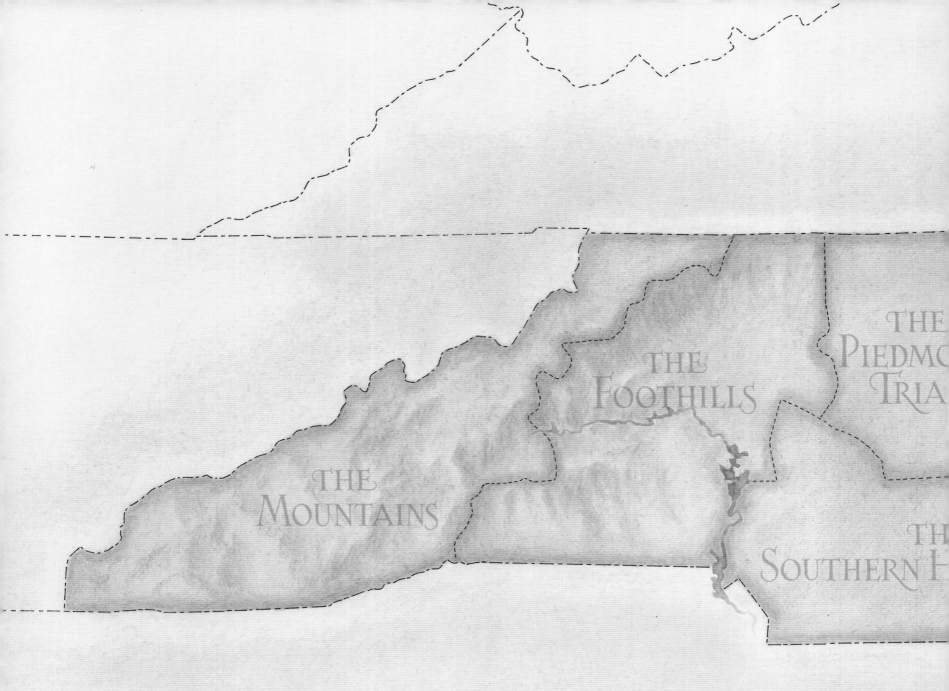

THE
PIEDM[O]
TRIA

THE
FOOTHILLS

THE
MOUNTAINS

TH[E]
SOUTHERN [H]

CHAPTER
THREE

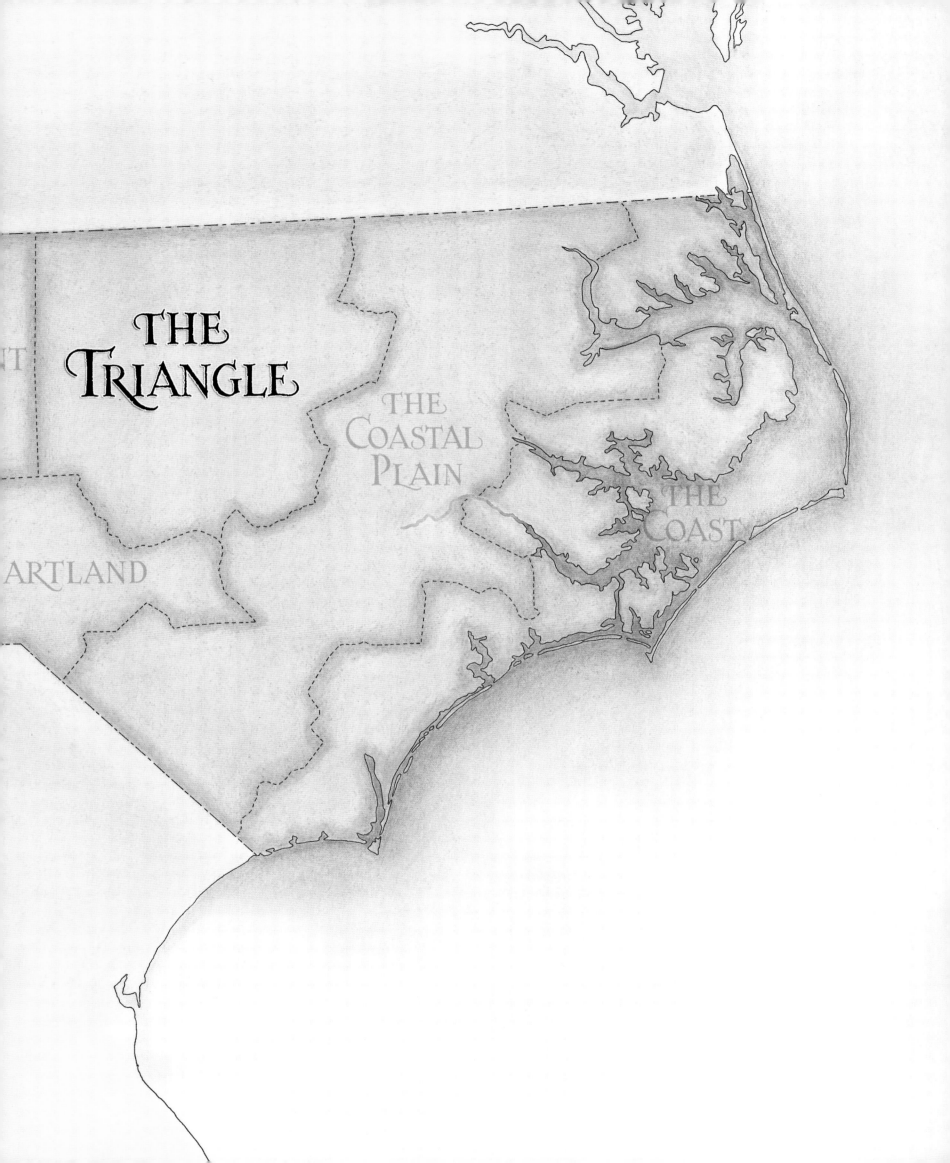

As Time Goes By
HANNAH'S CREEK PRIMITIVE BAPTIST CHURCH

It's been several years since services were held at Hannah's Creek Primitive Baptist Church, and the building is showing signs of abandonment. Window panes are broken out, and millions of flecks of white paint have popped off the wood siding.

Inside, a sad stillness blankets the sanctuary. Cobwebs float down from the bottom of pews; hymnals, 50-year-old hand fans, and mismatched seat cushions are mostly gathered in stacks on pews.

Built in the mid-19th century, Hannah's Creek is one of the few churches in North Carolina still laid out according to the meetinghouse plan, with the altar in the center of a long wall and surrounded on three sides by pews.

Pews on the east side of the altar were reserved for men (the men's side is identifiable by the presence of hat racks), while those on the west side were for women. The pews facing the front of the altar were called "neighbor pews." The building has three entrances, each opening to a particular set of pews.

Hannah's Creek Church was established in September 1817, and it flourished during the late 19th and early 20th centuries, as did other Primitive Baptist churches in the area. Thousands of people crowded the church grounds over a three-day period in September 1938, when Hannah's Creek played host to the meeting of the Little River Primitive Baptist Association.

By the mid-20th century, however, membership began declining, in part because of the denomination's difficulty in attracting young families, and in 2002 the church ceased having services.

In the cemetery, each tombstone tells a story. The epitaph of 14-year-old Nettie Parker, who died in 1924, declares, "In this little grave, worldwide hopes are buried." Soldiers killed in the Battle of Bentonville in 1865 are also believed to be buried here, but in unmarked graves. — *Kathy Grant Westbrook*

A Brave New World
ST. JOHN'S EPISCOPAL CHURCH

Location: **Williamsboro, Vance County**

Church Completed: **1773**

Worship: **Open for Special Services**

With anti-Crown protests growing hotter by the day, it was an awkward time for the Church of England to be building churches in the rebellious backcountry of North Carolina. But a few did get built, including St. John's Church, and it has sturdily survived a whole lot of history ever since.

The Williamsboro church was part of a bold new effort by the Anglicans to expand their presence westward into counties where the "dissenting" faiths — Quakers, Presbyterians, Baptists, Lutherans, and Reformed Germans — had already settled in. The newly established vestry began a handsome church in Hillsborough in 1768, and the next year fanned out to nearby Granville County to serve an area that included the wealthy plantation community of Nutbush (later renamed Williamsboro; Vance County was formed in 1881). Despite the local strength of Presbyterians and Baptists, missionary James McCartney baptized several hundred people, preached regularly, and saw hopes of building churches.

In the midst of this, however, political strife was engulfing the region and weakening support for the established church. Hillsborough and Granville County were hotbeds of the Regulators, and when Gov. William Tryon and his militia defeated the protesters in 1771, it did nothing to improve the popularity of Anglicanism here. Even so, only a few months later, the vestry pushed ahead with its church-building plan, and St. John's rose to completion in 1773.

With the American Revolution, the official church was dissolved and St. John's suffered from neglect for many years until the Episcopal Diocese of North Carolina was formed in the early 1800s. After the Raleigh and Gaston Railroad bypassed Williamsboro in 1840 and the town tapered off into a village, the church continued to survive as a country church with a small congregation.

St. John's fortunes shone again in the 1950s, when it underwent a thorough restoration and was reconsecrated. It is now used for special services. The original box pews, with their waist-high doors that once kept out winter drafts *(right)*, still bid worshipers a warm welcome. — *Mary Best*

The Bride of Christ
CONCORD UNITED METHODIST CHURCH

It's only a couple of minutes before the start of the Sunday morning worship service, but quiet has yet to fall over the sanctuary. The air is alive with chatting and bustling and laughter. A woman leans forward to the pew in front of her, encompassing its occupants in a group hug and showing off pictures of her grandchild. Two young men tarry in the center aisle, exchanging thoughts on the outcome of a recent football game. Several folks extend their hands in greeting to two strangers who have claimed the back pew. There is no doubt about it — the opportunity for fellowship is as important as the sermon at Concord United Methodist Church.

A generation ago, the congregation of Concord in northwest Person County was largely comprised of local farmers; today, the Rev. Randy Blanchard struggles to recall if there is even one farming family among the 270 members. Described as having evolved "from a community church into a transplant church," it is no longer filled only with natives of the Concord community but draws attendees from neighboring Roxboro and from the nearby burgeoning Hyco Lake area. Members agree that part of what makes this church special is that all feel welcome.

Although the birth of the church harkens to about 1815, the current sanctuary — the church's third — was built around 1908. The white, two-tower clapboard building is right at home in the rolling hills near the Virginia line. The view from the cemetery is one of old houses, fields, and a pond. An aura of timelessness envelops the surrounding countryside, disturbed only by power lines and a nearby gas station.

More than a dozen stained-glass windows line the sanctuary walls. So moved by them, during one of his sermons Blanchard invited members to stand in the pulpit some Sunday before or after a service to admire the windows from a different point of view. He asked that they appreciate the windows not just for their beauty but for the messages they deliver.

The church's stained glass also served as inspiration for a series of sermons preached by Blanchard. For the most part, he had no trouble preparing sermons based on the windows' familiar illustrations of such scenes as Jesus surrounded by children or praying in the Garden of Gethsemane.

But there was one notable exception. A window entitled *The Church Triumphant (right)* depicts a finely dressed woman holding a long palm leaf and a lamb. "Who was this woman?" Blanchard wondered. "What does this represent?" After conducting extensive research, he found the answer in several verses in the Book of Revelation, among them Chapter 19, verses 7-8: "Let us be glad and rejoice, and give honour to him: for the marriage of the Lamb is come, and his wife hath made herself ready. And to her was granted that she should be arrayed in fine linen, clean and white: for the fine linen is the righteousness of saints." This most unusual window illustrates the bride of Christ. — *Kathy Grant Westbrook*

Location: **Concord, Person County**

Current Church Completed: **1908**

Worship: **Regular Services**

All in a Day's Work
MILTON PRESBYTERIAN CHURCH

Visitors with an appreciation for Thomas Day will find much to marvel at in Milton Presbyterian Church. It was the church of the famous African-American cabinetmaker, and the sanctuary's graceful pews *(right)* are generally acknowledged to be examples of his handiwork. The handsome rosewood pulpit was possibly built by him as well.

Day was one of the wealthiest free men of color in North Carolina. Born in Virginia to free, property-owning parents, he moved as a young man to the town of Milton and soon had a thriving clientele for his elegant furniture and decorative woodworking. By the 1850s, Day's cabinetmaking shop was the largest in the state; he has been called an early founder of the modern Southern furniture industry.

Some stories claim he undertook the job of building his church's pews in exchange for being able to seat his family on the main floor, which traditionally was reserved for whites, rather than in the slave gallery. But historians consider this unlikely, given Day's stature in the congregation and community.

Milton was rather late getting its first church. Though established in 1796, the thriving wheat and tobacco trading center had no congregation until a group of women went about remedying the situation in 1825. They raised money to build a frame church near where the cemetery is now, then sponsored a subscription drive to hire a minister. Each donor had a vote in selecting the denomination. The Presbyterians had 38 votes, the Episcopalians eight. Thus, a Presbyterian minister was employed, and a congregation began. The choice was not surprising, for Presbyterianism had a long history in the county.

The Milton Presbyterians soon outgrew their first home, and in 1837 constructed the stylish brick church that sits on Broad Street near the center of town. Perched on a steep slope, it is built into the site to allow the portico and main entrance to open directly onto the street. Local lore has it that a disabled woman who lived across the street donated the land, so she would be able to roll her wheelchair right into church. — *Mary Best*

Location: **Milton, Caswell County**

Current Church Completed: **1837**

Worship: **Services Second and Fourth Sunday of the Month**

University Relations
THE CHAPEL OF THE CROSS

Situated squarely in the heart of Chapel Hill, on Franklin Street between the Morehead Planetarium and UNC's Spencer Dormitory, the Chapel of the Cross fosters and enjoys a close relationship with the students of the University of North Carolina.

The connection between church and college has existed for more than 150 years. The Rev. William Mercer Green, a professor at the university, presided over the organization of the parish in 1842. In 1848, when the congregation finally moved into its first church, five of the 22 communicants were UNC students.

The congregation outgrew its little church in the 1920s, but instead of tearing it down or moving, the church hired architect Hobart Upjohn to design a new Gothic Revival edifice and connect it to the old chapel via a cloister. The new church was completed in 1925.

The seriousness of the church's commitment to university outreach was evident in 1919 when the vestry fired its rector because he did not visit students often enough. In 1931, the Rev. Thomas Wright came to Chapel Hill to become a permanent chaplain for the students, and there has been someone in this role ever since.

The church basement has been home to the campus ministry since the 1950s. Every Tuesday night during the academic calendar, students gather for a hot meal followed by a worship service. A longtime tradition is the "stone soup" dinner available every night during exams, along with a quiet place to study.

The church has long acknowledged that living alongside an intellectually active university provides a wonderful environment for discussing moral and political issues, and its leaders have risen to the challenge. One of note was the Rev. David Yates, a pacifist who came to the church toward the end of World War II and worked to have a "prayer for our enemies" included in the prayer book. He also ensured that people of color were welcome to worship here.

In 1977, the Chapel of the Cross welcomed the Rev. Dr. Pauli Murray as she celebrated her first Eucharist after becoming the first black woman ordained to the Episcopal priesthood. For Murray and the church, it was a historic and poignant moment. A century and a half earlier, Murray's grandmother, a 10-year-old slave girl named Cornelia, was baptized in that very chapel.

The church's eagle lectern *(above)* was a gift from the diocese in memory of devout church leader Mary Ruffin Smith, who donated funds for the chapel's slate roof, a new organ, and church property. She brought young Cornelia here in 1854. — *Diane Silcox-Jarrett*

Location: **Chapel Hill, Orange County**

Current Church Completed: **1925**

Worship: **Regular Services**

The Blessing of History
ST. MATTHEW'S EPISCOPAL CHURCH

Location: **Hillsborough, Orange County**

Church Completed: **1826**

Worship: **Regular Services**

Quite possibly the oldest Gothic Revival church building still standing in North Carolina, St. Matthew's Episcopal Church in historic Hillsborough was completed in 1826, its design attributed to William Nichols who was state architect at the time.

Soon after the Civil War, the church began a series of renovations that were largely financed through the Women's Sewing Society, a group of church-women who made a successful business out of selling their handmade embroi-dery. The society, led by Lizzie Jones, was responsible for a remodeling of the building, including the raising of the roof, enlargement of the sanctuary to create space for the altar, the addition of a steeple, and the purchase of a pipe organ. The organ, bought in 1883, is still in use today.

The Sewing Society, which met weekly for 35 years, also made possible initial purchases of the church's unusual stained-glass windows. The brilliantly colored windows are dedicated to departed members; one 19th-century pane decorated with soft blue angels is a remembrance of Paul Carrington Cameron, who died at the age of three. Another window of note is the "Angel Window" *(right)*, which is made of Tiffany glass and was installed in 1899.

Hanging from the ceiling in the vestibule is a rope pulled each Sunday to ring the church bell. The bell was installed in 1878 as a mother's memorial to her son, a Confederate soldier, and to others who fell during the Civil War. The graves of soldiers dot the tranquil churchyard outside. — *Diane Silcox-Jarrett*

"A Great Towering Church"

DUKE CHAPEL

More than a decade before the 1935 dedication of majestic Duke Chapel, James B. Duke envisioned what a prominent, significant structure the building would be on the campus of Duke University. "I want the central building to be a church, a great towering church which will dominate all of the surrounding buildings," Duke said in 1924, "because such an edifice would be bound to have a profound influence on the spiritual life of the young men and women who come here."

Unfortunately, Duke didn't live long enough to see the fulfillment of his vision — he died in 1925 — but there's no question that Duke Chapel would have met the campus patriarch's expectations.

With its 73-foot interior ceiling and seating capacity of 1,800, Duke Chapel is one of the largest and most active university chapels in the United States. As for its significance, consider the following list of events that have taken place there: In addition to countless weddings, funerals, concerts, convocations, and baccalaureates, Duke Chapel has welcomed such well-known orators as the Rev. Billy Graham, American theologian Reinhold Niebuhr, and South African Nobel Peace Prize winner Desmond Tutu. Eleanor Roosevelt visited the chapel as first lady. And in 1950, the Dead Sea Scrolls were exhibited there.

Duke Chapel must be seen in person to appreciate it fully — not only its impressive size, but also the many other features that give it its character. In the main part of the chapel's interior, for example, 77 stained-glass windows made from more than a million pieces of glass depict about 800 saints and familiar characters and stories from the Old and New Testaments.

But perhaps even more magnificent, Duke Chapel features two organs — the original Aeolian organ, which was installed in and around the chancel when the chapel was built; and the Benjamin N. Duke Memorial Organ, a Flentrop instrument installed in 1976 over the chapel's entrance, which contains 5,033 speaking pipes. The Aeolian typically is used to accompany choirs, while the more impressive Flentrop provides the music for processionals and recessionals at major church services and during university events.

Finally, Duke Chapel's 210-foot-tall tower houses one of the finest carillons in the country, featuring 50 bells — ranging from a mere 10 pounds to a staggering 11,200 pounds. The carillon, first played in 1932, rings out across the campus at the end of each working day and during special events at the chapel.

If James B. Duke were around to see his chapel, it would probably give him chills. And he wouldn't be alone. — *Jimmy Tomlin*

Location: **Duke University, Durham, Durham County**

Church Completed: **1935**

Worship: **Regular Services and Special Campus Events**

A DREAM COME TRUE: A statue of industrialist and philanthropist James B. Duke stands in front of Duke Chapel to honor the man who envisioned and funded its grandeur. According to school records, he was so consumed with building the college that on his deathbed he said, "Don´t bother me, nurse. Today, I am laying out the university grounds." James, his brother Benjamin, and their father Washington are interred in the magnificent church's Memorial Chapel.

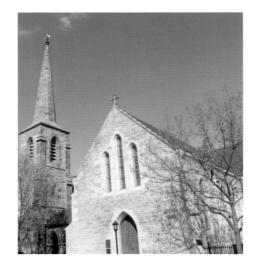

A Capital Treasure
CHRIST EPISCOPAL CHURCH

Location: **Raleigh,
Wake County**

Current Church Completed:
1861

Worship: **Regular Services**

A few years ago, Christ Episcopal Church underwent an extensive renovation that involved removing the floor of the chancel and digging up the ground beneath it. To everyone's surprise, the excavation also unearthed the answer to a long-hidden historical puzzle.

"We've found Bishop Ravenscroft!" was the immediate reaction of the building committee when diggers made contact with a stone object in the dirt. The crypt of John Stark Ravenscroft, the first consecrated Episcopal bishop of North Carolina and Christ Church's first rector, was finally found.

It had been known that the eminent clergyman was buried under the wooden church that was home to the congregation in 1830, the year he died — but no one could ever precisely locate his grave. A couple of decades later, that church was replaced with the stone church that stands at the center of North Carolina's capital today.

The discovery of the crypt was treated with reverence. A small group gathered to look and offer a prayer; then the stones were replaced. When the chancel project was completed, a small brass plaque was placed over the spot to mark for all time the resting place of the priest and bishop who began the work of the church nearly 180 years before.

Situated across from the State Capitol, Christ Church has always been held as an architectural treasure. Designed by renowned architect Richard Upjohn, the handsome building epitomizes the "Early English" Gothic style that came into vogue in the 1800s. The finishing touch is the gilded weathercock that stands atop the spire. A traditional symbol of the church, it also became the punch line in a witty Civil War–era observation. According to the story, after Raleigh was surrendered in 1865 and occupied by hungry Union troops, Christ Church's gilded cock was "the last chicken left in Raleigh." — *Mary Best*

City Counsel
FIRST BAPTIST CHURCH

Facing the North Carolina State Capitol from the northwest corner of Capitol Square, First Baptist Church shares an intimate relationship with the capital city of our state.

Twenty-three members — nine white and 14 black — organized Raleigh's first Baptist congregation in 1812 on the second floor of the old State House. Today, the distinguished English-style church, constructed in 1859 with its towering steeple and stuccoed walls *(right)*, continues to watch over the affairs of the Old North State.

But the church has not stood as a silent witness to North Carolina's past. Quite to the contrary, it has played a vital role, especially in wartime. During the Civil War, wounded Union and Confederate soldiers were cared for in the church basement and the church bell was melted down to make bullets for the Confederate army. Stories are also told of hidden tunnels dug during the war that supposedly still run from the church to the State Capitol building.

After the war, newly emancipated African-American members decided to form their own church. According to Bill Simpson, a lifetime member of First Baptist, "There was $1,000 in the church treasury at the time and it was split down the middle for the two congregations." Today, Raleigh continues to be home to two churches bearing the First Baptist name, and the two congregations share endeavors, such as helping the homeless and in the vocal ensemble, "First in Harmony."

The church did its part for the war effort during World War II as well. Members called the YMCA on weekends to invite soldiers in town on leave for a home-cooked meal and to attend Sunday worship services.

"One Christmas we had two fellows come to our house and the Y called and asked if we could take in another," remembered Frances Nipper, also a lifetime member of the church. "My father said 'sure' and went to get him. Two of the young men were Catholics, and they wanted to go to Mass on Christmas morning. It was snowing, but we all got ready and went with them."

In recent years, the 1,400-member church has focused on a different kind of agency. Among its various ministries, First Baptist is home to the downtown's first day-care center for infants and toddlers; it sponsors a mission church for Japanese people in the area and has the city's largest free-clothing center. — *Diane Silcox-Jarrett*

Location: **Raleigh, Wake County**

Current Church Completed: **1859**

Worship: **Regular Services**

All in the Family
HOLLAND'S UNITED METHODIST CHURCH

Location: **Raleigh, Wake County**

Current Church Completed: **2001**

Worship: **Regular Services**

When pious schoolmaster William Holland died childless in 1809 in southern Wake County, he bequeathed $400 "for the purpose of building a good Methodist Meeting House, that may have a partition at one end thereof for a classroom and to be built on such a piece of ground as will be convenient for my wife and the rest of the family to attend." In 1812, Sihon Smith, a local Methodist preacher, used the money to build a modest clapboard meetinghouse where he could fulfill his friend's dying wish.

Surely, Holland had no idea the vision he so carefully outlined would someday become a church home for hundreds of families in southern Wake County. The foundation he laid for the church's mission and focus on Christian education have remained integral parts of the church for its nearly 200-year history.

On any given Sunday at Holland United Methodist Church, the voices of young members can be heard singing in the choir, giving their testimony to the congregation, or laughing in the halls. Recently, that laughter has been enriched by six very special children from the former Soviet Union who have been adopted by church families. Two of the children — best friends — came from the same orphanage in the Republic of Georgia. Not wanting to separate the pair, the family returned for their second child in less than a year And in February 2004, the Rev. Keith Nanney *(above and right)* christened Chris and Deborah Baker's recently adopted Slavic child, Valentina Joy, into the church *(right)*.

The giving nature of Holland's rapidly growing congregation and the church's unwavering emphasis on the spiritual growth of children played a profound part in each family's decision to adopt, knowing their children would have two North Carolina families — their own and their church family at Holland's. — *Diane Silcox-Jarrett*

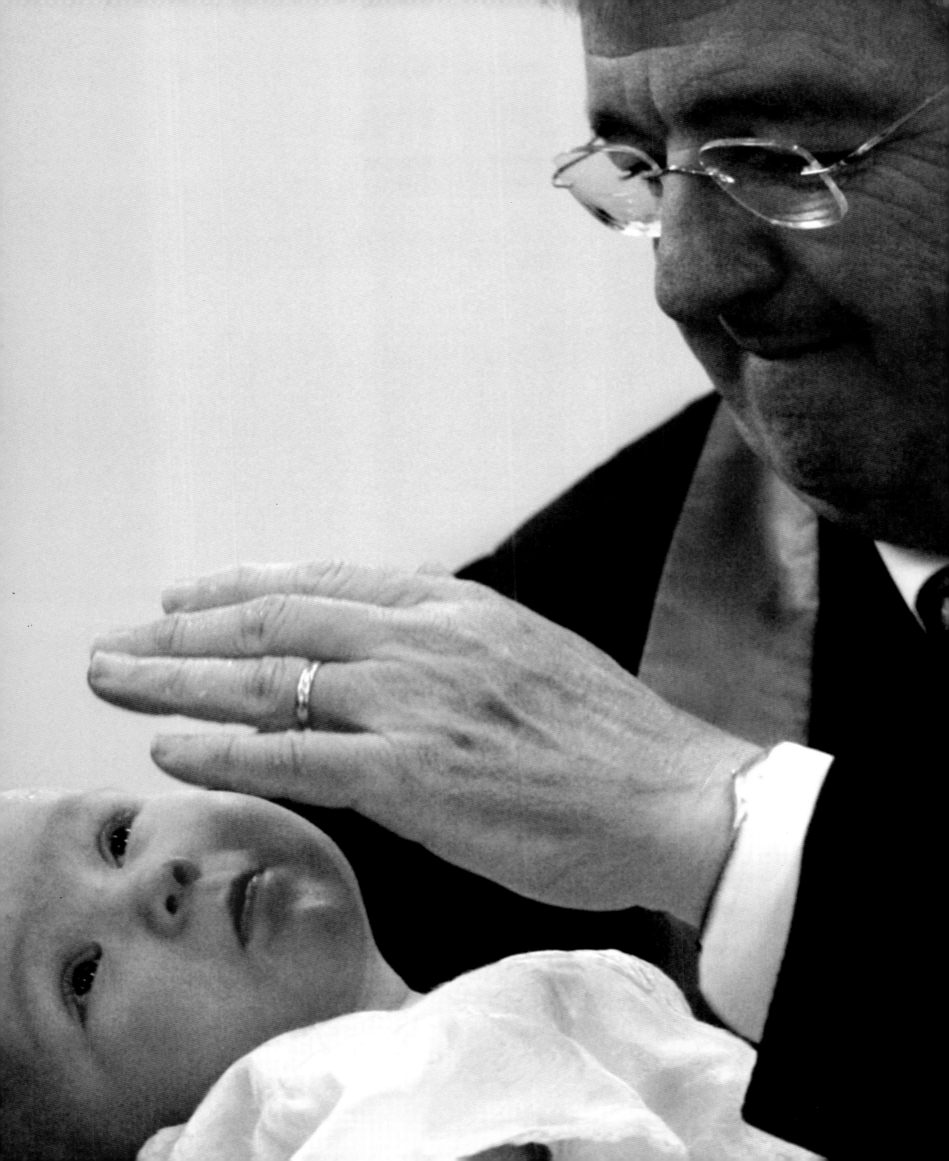

"Behold, I Stand at the Door ..." — *Revelation 3:20*
BARBECUE PRESBYTERIAN CHURCH

On a cold winter's night in 1766, a stranger stumbled upon a small log building in the community of Barbecue. Having battled the season's fiercest elements, he must have been relieved to find shelter from the raging storm. But the door was locked, and when he knocked, there came no answer.

No one could say how long the stranger lingered there, or how he had come upon it in the first place. All the locals knew was that when they found him the next morning on the steps of the building — the recently constructed Barbecue Church — he was dead. He had frozen to death. He became the first person to be buried in the church cemetery (*right*).

The stranger's plight inspired an unusual legacy of this Harnett County institution: The doors of the church remain open around the clock, lest another stranger needing warmth — or a place to pray — should happen along. Only the pastor's study and the fellowship hall are locked. "The front door is always unlocked," said Laura Shaw Cameron, a longtime member and historian of what is now Barbecue Presbyterian Church.

Formally organized in 1758 by Scottish settlers, the church adopted its Barbecue moniker from nearby Barbecue Creek — named because morning mist rising off the water reminded early immigrants of the smoky barbecue pits they had seen in the West Indies.

The church's first preacher was the Rev. James Campbell, a Scottish-born clergyman who came to North Carolina from Pennsylvania. Early services were preached in both English and Gaelic, the native tongue of the Scottish Highlanders. Campbell was called by three area churches — Barbecue, Bluff, and Longstreet. It is believed that he was the first preacher ever called to serve churches in North Carolina who actually stayed, according to Cameron.

It wasn't until 1765 that the congregation constructed its first church, the log meetinghouse. A larger church was constructed in 1775. The third church, which is the present sanctuary, was built in 1896 and has undergone a number of renovations and additions, most recently in the 1990s.

The story of the stranger is only one chapter in the church's colorful history. Around 1771, among those who attended the church regularly was Scottish heroine Flora MacDonald, known for having come to the aid of Scotland's Bonnie Prince Charlie. She lived in the area for nine months or so and worshiped at Barbecue Church. A "Cairn of Remembrance" — stones piled up as a memorial, in the tradition of the Old Testament — was built on the church grounds and includes stone from MacDonald's homestead in Scotland.

Barbecue Church has stood as a symbol of faith that not only soars during good times, but also endures the tough times. In 1835, the church had lost so many members to daughter churches in the area that the Fayetteville Presbytery met to dissolve it. Barbecue was saved, however, when the Rev. Colin McIver proclaimed, "No! No! I will serve her! Without money and price if necessary!" He became Barbecue's pastor in 1839 and served another decade, during which time the church thrived under his leadership.

Now, nearly 250 years after its founding, the historic church stands as strong as ever. — *Jimmy Tomlin*

Location: **Barbecue, Harnett County**

Current Church Completed: **1896**

Worship: **Regular Services**

SACRED
TO THE MEMORY OF
A STRANGER
1766

THE
PIEDMO
TRIAI

THE
FOOTHILLS

THE
MOUNTAINS

TH
SOUTHERN H

CHAPTER
FOUR

THE
TRIANGLE

THE
COASTAL
PLAIN

THE
COAST

EARTLAND

How Firm the Foundation
OLD BLUFF PRESBYTERIAN CHURCH

Beneath a flawless blue sky, long rows of tombstones and tall stands of trees materialize almost out of nowhere. Move closer, and a glimpse of white peeks through; closer still, and a red roof appears. Old Bluff Presbyterian Church stands in a clearing behind the tombstones and trees, in one of the most tranquil settings in Cumberland County. Even on Sunday mornings, a soft silence cloaks the old building, the congregation having departed in 1908.

The Greek Revival–style building is beautifully maintained, nonetheless, along with its cemetery and grounds, by the Old Bluff Presbyterian Church Trust. Everything below the red roof — siding, molding, columns, doors, bench on the porch, even window panes — appears washed in white; the church almost glows in the morning sunlight. Built in the 1850s, this was the third building to house the Presbyterian congregation and was entered in the National Register of Historic Places in 1974.

Sitting on a high bluff above the Cape Fear River about two miles north of the town of Wade, Old Bluff is one of the oldest churches in the Upper Cape Fear Valley, founded by Scottish immigrants in the 1750s. When the fledgling congregation petitioned their native country for a missionary to serve them, they met with no success. But when they petitioned the Presbytery of Philadelphia, the Rev. James Campbell answered the call. Campbell, a Scottish Highlander who came to North Carolina around 1757, was the first Presbyterian minister to settle in this area, also establishing the Longstreet and Barbecue Presbyterian churches. Campbell preached in both English and Gaelic; in fact, services at Old Bluff were conducted in Gaelic for nearly 100 years.

A monument honoring Campbell stands on the church grounds. Words etched into its surface describe him as "a wise and pure Patriot, a faithful defender of the principles of the Presbyterian Church, a zealous Preacher of the Gospel, a devout and humble Christian." Although now praised for his patriotic zeal, Campbell's support of American independence from England was unpopular with his mostly Loyalist congregation. His views so rankled church members that he was forced to leave Old Bluff and move to Guilford County. It was only after independence was won that he returned to his home on the west bank of the Cape Fear, where he died in 1780. Although he is not buried at Old Bluff, his daughter, Lovday, rests here.

Beginning in the 1890s, members of Old Bluff left to form other congregations; finally the remaining congregation moved to Wade to become Bluff Presbyterian Church.

Even though its pulpit stands empty on Sunday mornings, Old Bluff is not forgotten. The church is used occasionally for weddings and funerals, and every year on the fourth Sunday in September, members of Old Bluff's three daughter churches gather for a homecoming with singing, dinner on the grounds, and bagpipe music. It is one day when Old Bluff is not enveloped in silence. — *Kathy Grant Westbrook*

Location: **Wade, Cumberland County**

Church Completed: **1850s**

Worship: **Open for Special Services and Annual Homecoming**

"People Came by the Thousands"
LITTLE TABERNACLE

Location: **Falcon, Cumberland County**

Church Completed: **1898**

Worship: **Open for Camp Meetings and Special Services**

Humble in appearance, the Little Tabernacle looms large in the history of the Pentecostal Holiness Church. It was in this eight-sided building that the more than 3.2 million-member international Christian denomination was born in 1911 with the official merger of the Fire Baptized Holiness Church and the Pentecostal Holiness Church.

The tabernacle's builder was Julius Culbreth, who grew up a Methodist near the town of Dunn. His life took a different turn in 1896, however, when he and his wife attended a tent revival and were saved. His octagonal building memorializes the sacred spot where they dedicated their lives to God.

Culbreth (who also is credited with giving the town of Falcon its name, after a brand of writing pens) constructed the little chapel in 1898 from the wood of pine trees knocked down during a tornado. With its completion, folks in the northeastern corner of Cumberland County had a place to hold nondenominational prayer meetings, and two years later, their benefactor organized the first Falcon Camp Meeting.

The early camp meetings had no amenities and no running water, except for the nearby Black River. Still, Culbreth noted, "people came by the thousands from near and far on buggies, wagons, dump carts drawn by horses, mules and oxen … sleeping in small tents or under trees." The meeting became an annual event and is still held today.

After the Pentecostal congregation outgrew the octagonal church and moved to a new facility, it was used as a schoolhouse and, in the 1920s, for storage. In 1943, however, the tabernacle was refurbished and a porch added to the front door. In 1947, it got its first Hammond organ. In 1952, after construction of Culbreth Memorial Church, it was used for Sunday school and later as an educational building.

During the 1980s, the Rev. J.D. Lee led a campaign to have the tabernacle placed on the National Register of Historic Places. The building has been moved to a prominent place in town atop a hill on the main thoroughfare through Falcon, a picturesque setting popular for special occasions. — *David La Vere*

Windows to the Soul
ST. JOHN'S EPISCOPAL CHURCH

Location: **Fayetteville, Cumberland County**

Current Church Completed: **1832**

Worship: **Regular Services**

When the Rev. Joseph Caldwell Huske, the longest-serving rector of St. John's Episcopal, gazed down upon Cross Creek from the church vestry in the 1800s, he compared the stream to the flow of human life, saying, "… as it hurries on, never stopping from one years [sic] end to another, it reminds me of the rapid flow of all human life, onward and ever onward, towards the Ocean of Eternity!" So, too, can the stream be likened to the life of St. John's Church, moving "onward and ever onward."

Formally organized on April 7, 1817, as the first Episcopal church in Fayetteville, St. John's has since given rise to all other Episcopal churches in the city. When their first church burned in 1831, the congregation quickly rebuilt on the same foundation, introducing the city to Neo-Gothic architecture. Ten pyramidal spires and lancet windows give the stunning stuccoed brick structure a castle-like appearance *(above)*.

St. John's beauty is enhanced by its resplendent stained glass. In 1890, three memorial windows were installed in the sanctuary. One directly above the altar depicts the church's patron saint while the other two, positioned on either side, portray St. Paul and St. Timothy. From 1899 to 1902, eight additional stained-glass windows, exquisitely crafted in Munich, Germany, were installed in the nave *(right)*. Each window consists of two distinct sections: The bottom portion with a pictorial representation of the New Testament illuminates the church's main level, while the top portion, composed of a decorative design, glimmers along the balcony level. — *Kathy Grant Westbrook*

A Founding Father

EVANS METROPOLITAN A.M.E. ZION CHURCH

The white cross built into the front gable *(above)* of Evans Metropolitan A.M.E. Zion Church is decidedly askew, representing the struggles encountered by Henry Evans as he worked to establish the Fayetteville church.

During the late 1700s, Evans, a free black shoemaker and an ordained Methodist minister, arrived in Fayetteville en route to Charleston, South Carolina, from his home in Virginia. Deeply disturbed by the conduct of local slaves, which he attributed to a lack of scriptural guidance, he decided to stay and preach to the black population.

His immediate success preaching to the slaves worried their white owners, who fretted about the influence Evans wielded. As opposition to the minister mounted, he was accused of not only inciting rebellion among local slaves, but also being a runaway slave himself. The town council ordered him to desist from preaching, but he was undeterred and continued delivering his sermons, albeit cautiously. Eventually, a mob of local citizens tried unsuccessfully to put an end to Evans' ministry. But he refused to relent, even reputedly swimming across the icy waters of the Cape Fear River on occasion to deliver his message out of reach of his persecutors.

The tide turned for Evans when slave owners heard his dynamic preaching style; his powerful message elicited in them a spiritual awakening. The African Meeting House he built on Cool Spring Street in 1796 — Fayetteville's first church building — soon overflowed with black and white congregants. Formally organized in 1801, the church was enthusiastically attended by members of both races.

In 1806, the meetinghouse burned, but was rebuilt. Four years later, Evans died. In 1831, fire swept through Fayetteville, destroying Evans' second church building. The congregation, now numbering more than 300 blacks and nearly 150 whites, moved to Hay Street. Around 1855, black members returned to Cool Spring Street and constructed a third building, which also was lost to fire.

In 1893, Evans Metropolitan A.M.E. Zion Church built its current building. A tablet on the basement floor of the brick church, surrounded by a wrought iron railing, indicates the final resting place of Henry Evans, hailed as the father of Methodism in eastern North Carolina. Upstairs in the sanctuary, the pulpit is directly above where Evans is entombed. — *Kathy Grant Westbrook*

Location: **Fayetteville, Cumberland County**

Current Church Completed: **1893**

Worship **Regular Services**

Where Heroes Worship

FORT BRAGG'S POST CHAPELS

A symbol of American might, Fort Bragg cares for the spiritual strength of nearly 55,000 soldiers and their families stationed at the sprawling U.S. Army complex in no fewer than 10 houses of worship.

Taking center stage is the Main Post Chapel *(left)*, adjacent to the Main Post Parade Field. Construction of the nonsectarian chapel began in 1932, and it was officially completed on March 9, 1935. (Fort Bragg was founded in 1918.)

Built of stucco with a Spanish-Revival–style roof and classical tower, the Main Post Chapel seats about 300 people. Built at a cost of a little more than $69,000, "it represents one of the first times the U.S. government funded a military religious building," noted base historian Donna Tabor.

The Main Post Chapel's powerful stained-glass windows were handcrafted from more than 14,000 tiny pieces of antique glass from around the world and installed in 1945. Containing more than 1,000 pieces alone, the center window directly behind the altar illustrates an American eagle and the motto "In God We Trust" *(page 121)*.

Another well-known chapel at Fort Bragg is the JFK Memorial Chapel, built in 1966 on Ardennes Street. The chapel, of course, is named for John F. Kennedy, the 35th president of the United States, who was regarded as the "patron" of Special Forces soldiers. The chapel is recognized for its stunning stained-glass windows, which depict Special Forces soldiers in action, as well as patriotic and biblical military campaigns. In the front of the chapel is a special monument from movie legend John Wayne as an expression of gratitude to the Special Forces for their help during filming of the Vietnam War movie *The Green Berets*.

Other highlights of the base's chapels include the 82nd Airborne Division Memorial Chapel, which features stained-glass windows depicting various military campaigns, and the Wood Memorial Chapel, named in memory of George B. Wood, a chaplain who was assigned to the 505th Parachute Infantry Regiment of the 82nd Airborne Division and is believed to be the only chaplain in World War II who made four combat jumps. — *Jimmy Tomlin*

Location: **Fort Bragg, Cumberland County**

Main Chapel Completed: **1935**

Worship: **Regular Services for Various Denominations, with Limited Access to the Base**

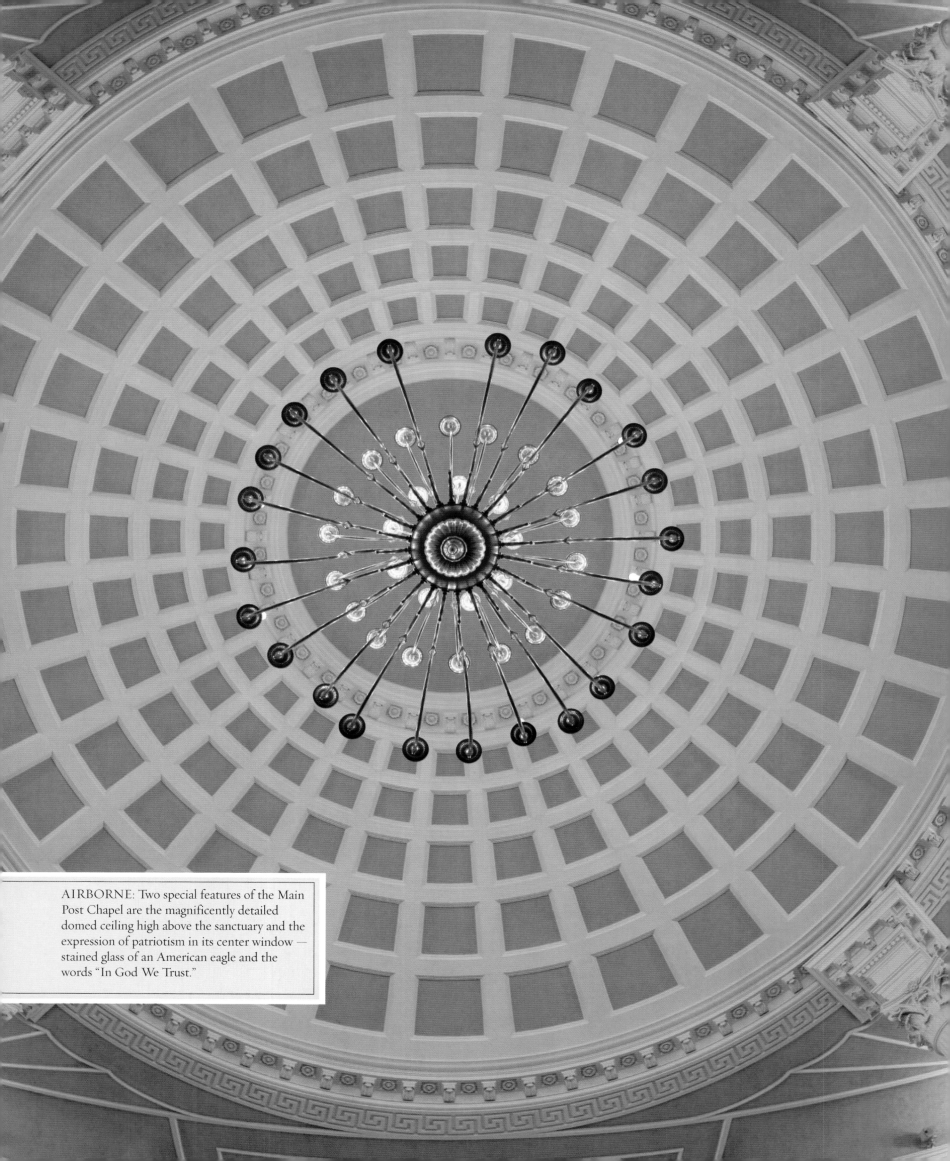

AIRBORNE: Two special features of the Main
Post Chapel are the magnificently detailed
domed ceiling high above the sanctuary and the
expression of patriotism in its center window —
stained glass of an American eagle and the
words "In God We Trust."

Sanctuary Under the Pines
VILLAGE CHAPEL

Perhaps it was inevitable that historic Pinehurst would have a place of worship shared by people of different faiths; after all, this was the dream of the golf village's founder, Bostonian James Walker Tufts. To make his dream a reality, he invited his good friend, author and Unitarian minister Dr. Edward Everett Hale of Boston, to come to the newly established model resort village in 1896 to preach. The two accomplished men shared a vision of a community and church in which people of all denominations could live and worship together.

The results were astounding, leading to the formation of the Pinehurst Religious Association. During the early 1900s, the group met initially in the town hall, but soon the Tufts family donated what church minister Dr. Thaddeus A. Cheatham described as "the choicest site in Pinehurst" on which to build a chapel to house their interdenominational congregation. Eminent architect Hobart Upjohn designed the charming chapel. The church held its inaugural worship service on March 1, 1925.

At its very heart, the Village Chapel has remained true to its profound mission of Christian fellowship and to the lighter, more earthly ideals of its links community. In his history of the church, Cheatham wrote, "Into the cornerstone was placed a Bible, a Prayer Book, current copies of the local newspapers, maps of the four golf courses in Pinehurst and, by decision of the Board, a certified copy of the minister's best score, a 74 on the No. 2 course, a little jest to give a sort of Pinehurst flavor." An impressive score on all counts.

Today, the chapel remains true to Tufts' vision — it is unquestionably interdenominational, governed by a board of directors whose members represent a variety of faiths. To accommodate the needs of a diverse congregation, the chapel offers a variety of services every Sunday morning. — *Kathy Grant Westbrook*

Location: **Pinehurst, Moore County**

Church Completed: **1925**

Worship: **Regular Services**

O Come, All Ye Faithful
SHILOH METHODIST CHURCH

When Montgomery County old-timers speak of Shiloh Methodist Church, they speak of a place that once played host to some of the most joyous worship services this side of heaven. Rock-ribbed preaching, beloved hymns, and the sweet communion of fellowship characterized the historic one-room meetinghouse, which stands in an oak grove about a mile north of Troy.

Unfortunately, the old, rugged church stands empty now. Sunday mornings come and go, but Shiloh remains still — a silent witness to the vibrant worship services that took place here generations ago.

More than 75 years after Shiloh closed, however, the old church still draws the community faithful together — not only as a historic landmark but also as a house of worship. Twice a year visitors flock to Shiloh for special services. During the fall, they gather for the annual Shiloh reunion, a daylong celebration that includes a morning worship, a picnic on the grounds, and fellowship. On the first Saturday in December, they come for the annual Shiloh Christmas Candlelight Tea and Communion, which features refreshments, holiday music, the reading of the Christmas story, and communion. For the celebration, volunteers deck the halls of the sanctuary in early 20th-century yuletide fare *(right)*.

Those who still come to the weathered church — many of whose ancestors were members — do so because it is a bridge to the past. Others say that Shiloh, which means "place where God dwells," gives them an inner peace. "You go there and get this sense of serenity," said Brenda Byrd, a member of the Shiloh Memorial Association, which in 1967 took ownership of the church property. "Shiloh kind of takes you back to the 1800s and the early 1900s."

Shiloh's rich history dates to the early 1800s, if not earlier, and the church remained an active house of worship until it was unceremoniously closed in 1928 by the North Carolina Methodist Conference. Members scattered to other churches throughout the community, but they never forgot about Shiloh. Within a few years, discussions began about a reunion, the first being held in 1939. It became an annual event and remains a well-attended gathering each September.

Although the church is not open, it still provides spiritual comfort to visitors who frequently come for a quiet moment's rest on benches outside the church and near the cemetery. — *Jimmy Tomlin*

Location: **Troy, Montgomery County**

Current Church Completed: **1883**

Worship: **Open for Annual Reunion and Christmas Tea**

"For Christ in the Heart of Charlotte"
FIRST PRESBYTERIAN CHURCH

Location: **Charlotte, Mecklenburg County**

Current Church Completed: **1857**

Worship: **Regular Services**

Organized in 1821 as the Queen City's first church, First Presbyterian Church holds a commanding presence in Uptown Charlotte. The shaded church complex stretches a full city block between Trade and Church streets, rubbing shoulders with homes in Fourth Ward, titan towers of finance, and the thriving commercial district of North Carolina's largest city.

Scots-Irish Presbyterians acquired the property in 1835, and the congregation quickly outgrew its first church. A second building was erected on the site in 1857 — a brick structure in grand Gothic Revival style — and its architectural style has been retained in subsequent additions. Inside, sterling silver chandeliers and Tiffany stained glass illuminate the sprawling sanctuary.

During the Civil War, Confederates wanted to melt down the church bell for ammunition, but Charlotteans voted to melt the town bell instead. The First Presbyterian bell was then placed in the courthouse tower, where it tolled for the town until 1942 when it was returned to the church.

First Presbyterian's contributions to Charlotte have been much more than architectural. As part of its commitment to be "For Christ in the Heart of Charlotte," it has been a mainstay for those who live and work downtown, as well as an influence in the lives of the city's youngest residents. In 1947, the church opened Charlotte's first child enrichment center for working mothers. In 1969, it began offering piano lessons to children who could not afford them otherwise. Before long the idea of putting slightly used pianos to use during the week turned into the Community School of the Arts and now serves several thousand students with 30 to 40 locations throughout the city. — *Diane Silcox-Jarrett*

Heroes and Heritage
HOPEWELL PRESBYTERIAN CHURCH

The names of Alexander, Cathey, Davidson, Latta, McDonald, and McGrady have been on the membership rolls of Hopewell Presbyterian Church for many generations. Those good old Scots-Irish names blend with the church's colonial American pedigree to fill Hopewell with tradition, ritual, and legend.

Among the most popular stories is that of local Revolutionary War hero Gen. William Lee Davidson, who was buried at Hopewell after falling at the Battle of Cowan's Ford in 1781. (Davidson College was named in his honor.) Two Hopewell members rescued Davidson's body, which was found "plundered and stripped of every garment" on the banks of the Catawba River. Knowing they could not get to Davidson's home church because of advancing British forces, they brought the body to Hopewell and sent for his young widow so she could attend her husband's funeral. "This story reflects the mettle of the congregation," said the Rev. Jeff Lowrance. "It shows Hopewell's character during a critical time in history."

One of the seven original Presbyterian churches in Mecklenburg County, Hopewell was organized around 1760 by the Rev. Alexander Craighead, a missionary and patriot known as the "father of the American Revolution in Mecklenburg County." Five members of Hopewell signed the Mecklenburg Declaration of Independence. The current church building, its earliest sections constructed in 1833, is considered one of the oldest and finest Federal style churches in Mecklenburg County.

One unusual feature of the church's sanctuary is a wall clock, which has faced the congregation since the 1870s. According to Tina Brown, chair of Hopewell's historical committee, "We have always teased our ministers that the deacons back then must have put the clock facing the congregation so they could tell the pastor if he was talking too long."

Along with its American roots, Hopewell celebrates its Celtic heritage as well *(right)*. Each December, Hopewell holds an ambitious Celtic Christmas program that features traditional Celtic music, including bagpipes and Irish flute; a medieval English shepherd's play performed by children of the congregation; Scottish dancing; traditional dress; and stories read in Gaelic, Welsh, and Scottish.

In the fellowship hall, 52 tartans hang from the ceiling — their majestic colors tell of Scottish family pride and show support for the church. On Heritage Sunday every October, members take the tartans down and march them into the sanctuary to be blessed. Bagpipes are played, men wear kilts and tam-o'-shanters, and the names of Scottish forefathers are read so all can reflect on those who helped sustain the church. — *Diane Silcox-Jarrett*

Location: **Huntersville, Mecklenburg County**

Current Church Completed: **1833**

Worship: **Regular Services**

Soldiers of the Cross
SOLDIERS MEMORIAL A.M.E. ZION CHURCH

Location: **Salisbury, Rowan County**

Current Church Completed: **1913**

Worship: **Regular Services**

In 1796, a group of black Methodists in New York formed a breakaway denomination. In the decades that followed, the movement spread, and in 1864, it took root in the town of Salisbury.

Soldiers Memorial A.M.E. Zion Church began with prayers and discussions by three African-American men meeting in a boot shop, with the fledgling congregation later moving to the Freedmen's Building on East Council Street. Their first home was destroyed in a storm in 1867. They rebuilt, but a windstorm in 1886 obliterated that building, too. Completed in 1913 on Church Street, the existing brick church reflects the Gothic Revival architecture seen in many A.M.E. Zion churches. A large arched stained-glass window serves as a centerpiece of the spacious, red-carpeted sanctuary.

The church's history is indelibly mingled with that of Livingstone College, founded in 1879 by Soldiers Memorial minister-member Dr. Joseph Charles Price, a giant in the history of the A.M.E. Zion movement. The college, still affiliated today with the denomination, was started as an educational institution for aspiring black clergy. During his tenure as president of Livingstone, Price required the student body to attend services, and he encouraged the church to take an active interest in the cultivation of the students.

Price's friend the Rev. William Harvey Goler continued and expanded the legacy. A pastor at Soldiers Memorial from 1885 to 1888, he founded Hood Theological Seminary and served as Livingstone's second president after Price's death in 1893. Members credit him for giving impetus to the church. It was his proposal to rename it in honor of the Union soldiers who delivered their emancipation.

The church celebrated the 140th anniversary of its founding in 2004 with a service honoring the life and legacy of Price, and as a usual occurrence, Livingstone College students took part in the program. — *Keith McKenzie*

Rock of Ages
ZION (ORGAN) LUTHERAN CHURCH

Spurred by the success of settlers before them and the availability of fertile, cheap land in North Carolina, German immigrants moved to Rowan County and surrounding areas from Pennsylvania in the middle of the 18th century. Some were members of the Lutheran Church; others, the Reformed Church. Known for their sober-sided practicality, both sets of pioneers put their faith in stone.

In the early years, the two groups shared a single house of worship, a simple wooden meetinghouse they called Hickory Church. By the 1790s, however, both set forth in building the massive granite structures that stand yet today.

Zion Lutheran Church is the older of Rockwell's two stone churches and the oldest Lutheran church in the state, completed about 1794-1795. Its familiar name of Organ Church dates to 1786, when Johannes Steigerwalt caused a sensation by building the congregation a beloved pipe organ — a unique addition for a frontier church at the time. Ensconced in the gallery of the new meetinghouse, the organ remained in use for nearly 100 years.

One of the most colorful chapters in Organ Church history and proof of its resilience came in 1825 when the "Henkelites," disgruntled members of a breakaway Lutheran synod in Tennessee begun by David Henkel, tried to seize control of the property — first by making a copy of the door key and then by hiding under the pews after communion one Saturday evening. The Henkelites were bodily ousted, and the North Carolina Supreme Court eventually settled the controversy in the church's favor. Over time, the congregation regained its harmony.

Members moved into a larger church building in 1960, and keeping with the tradition of its musical name, boasts a magnificent organ of 1,814 pipes. The old chapel is still in good repair, and early services are held within its old walls during the summer. — *Keith McKenzie*

Location: **Rockwell, Rowan County**

Original Church Completed: **1794-1795**

Worship: **Occasional Services Held in the Original Church; Regular Services in Newer Sanctuary**

"For by Grace Are Ye Saved" — *Ephesians 2:8*
GRACE EVANGELICAL AND REFORMED
(LOWER STONE) CHURCH

**Location: Rockwell,
Rowan County**

Original Church Completed:
1795

Worship: **Regular Services;
Now a Member of the
United Church of Christ**

Grace Evangelical and Reformed Church is known locally as Lower
Stone, and that's because of where it is situated — just down the
road from Zion Lutheran Church, another massive stone church
built by German immigrants in the late 18th century.

Construction of Lower Stone began in 1795 and came in stages, perhaps wall
by wall. Over the north, south, and west doorways are tablets with German
inscriptions. The south wall bears the image of a clock with the time 9:30 etched
above the face and the inscription "In the year of Christ, 1795: with God's help."
The church was dedicated in 1817. A bell tower was added to the roof in 1901.

The sycamore tree that stands near the church *(right)* is a precious part of its
history. Legend has it that the tree grew from a wooden stake that had been
driven into the ground as a marker when the church was being built. In 1975,
the tree was hit by lightning and the congregation had to make a decision about
whether to cut it down. They chose, instead, to do whatever was needed to preserve and tend to the health of their old neighbor. And it stands there still.

Surrounded by gray gravestones in the old churchyard, Lower Stone stands
sturdy alongside the sycamore. Members pass through the same south door of
their German ancestors. Just above, the inscription reads (English translation):
"To the Glory of God has been built, the church which you behold ..."

Lower Stone Church has been the mother church for the formation of
other Reformed churches in the area. Since 1957, it has been a full member of
the United Church of Christ. — *Keith McKenzie*

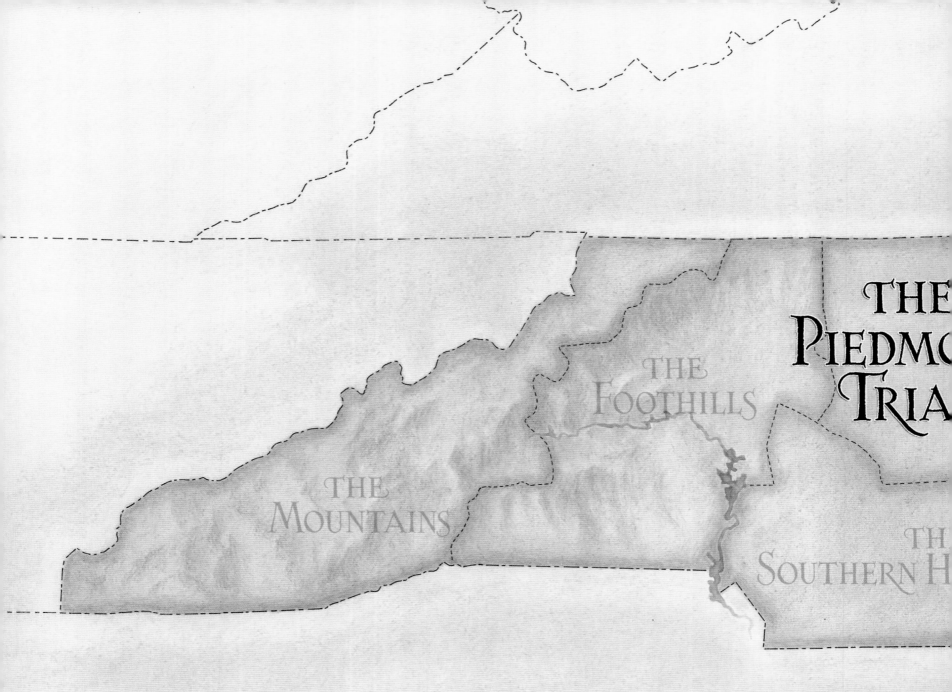

THE
PIEDMO
TRIA

THE
Foothills

THE
MOUNTAINS

THE
SOUTHERN H

CHAPTER
FIVE

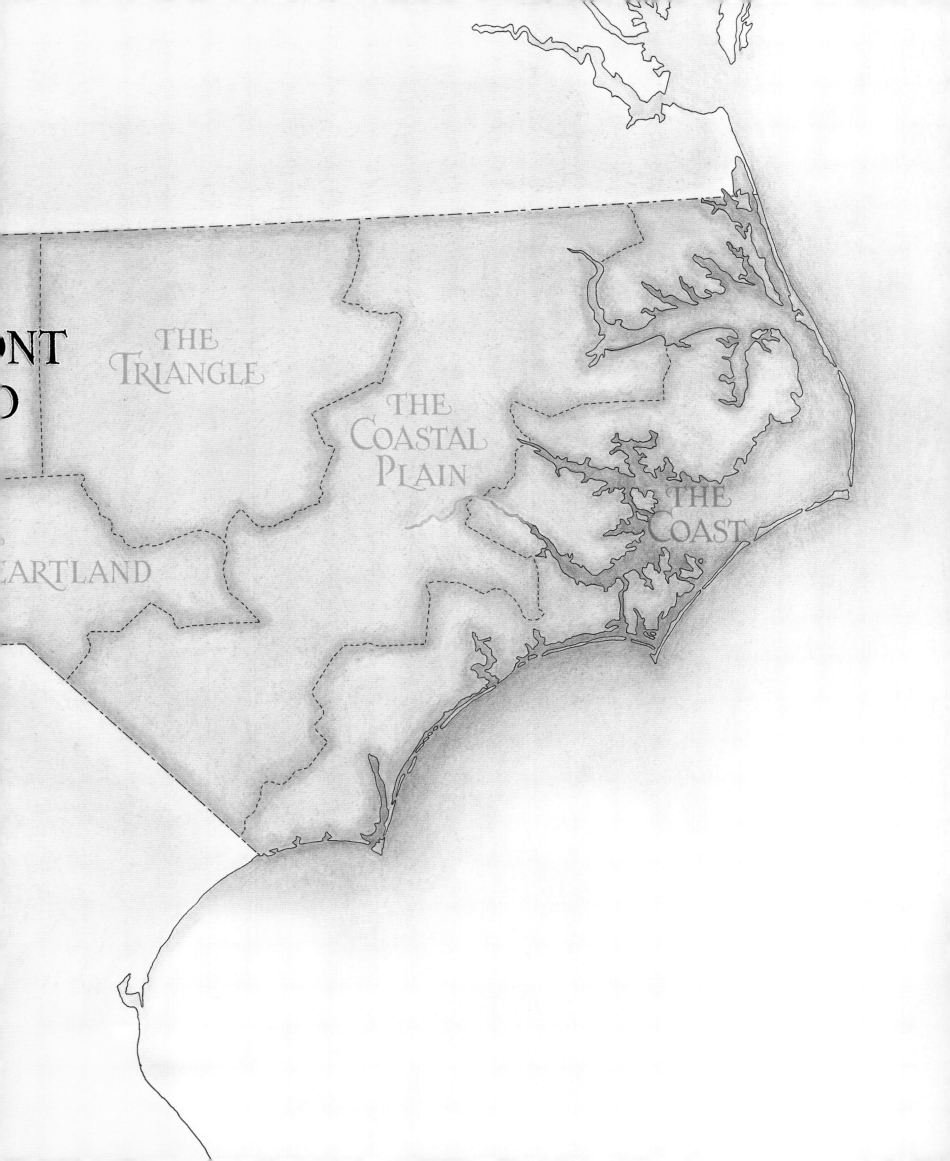

A Mighty Fortress
FIRST PRESBYTERIAN CHURCH

Location: **Greensboro, Guilford County**

Current Church Completed: **1929**

Worship: **Regular Services**

A tower of spiritual and architectural strength, First Presbyterian grew from an initial gathering of 12 souls in 1824, when Greensboro had no churches and it is believed to have had only two professing two professing Christians among its population of two-dozen families. (While First Presbyterian was the first congregation to meet within the city limits, Buffalo Presbyterian and Alamance Presbyterian had been established in Guilford County more than a half century earlier.) The racially diverse congregation organized by the Rev. William Denny Paisley reflected the reality of their day: There were eight white members and four black members, and the black members were all slaves.

The church grew steadily and built its first house of worship in 1830 at the corner of Davie and Church streets in downtown Greensboro. Fourteen years later, a larger church took its place on the site. In 1849, the congregation installed its first organ — and it was the town's only organ for 50 years.

Caught up in the Civil War, First Presbyterian answered the call to service. As the Union Army advanced and the South braced for a stand against General Sherman, the church donated its bell to the Confederacy to be melted down for bullets. In the last dark stages of the war in 1865, the church became a hospital for wounded soldiers.

The congregation has been in its current home overlooking Fisher Park since 1929. It is a medieval-appearing brick sentinel modeled after the "Fortress Gothic" architecture of the 13th-century Cathedral of St. Cecelia in Albi, France. A 25-foot rose window, resplendent in blue stained glass, frames the immense, soaring interior. At the center of the huge window is a portrayal of Christ seated on His throne, hands uplifted to signify "I am with you always." In a corner of the sanctuary, a stained-glass window depicting the Star of David and the Scales of Justice presents a neighborly face to Temple Emanuel, Greensboro's oldest Jewish temple across the street. — *Keith McKenzie*

A Mother's Love
OUR LADY OF GRACE CATHOLIC CHURCH

Named in tribute to the mother of Jesus, Our Lady of Grace Catholic Church also stands as a memorial to another beloved and devout lady. The soaring, pink granite church is a legacy of love for Ethel Clay Price from her husband and children.

Ethel Clay Price had converted to Catholicism as a student at Notre Dame Academy in Maryland and she held devoutly to her faith, even though the man she wed in 1897 was a Baptist and they went to live in a city of few Catholics, Greensboro. Her husband, Julian Price, honored her beliefs throughout their years together, welcoming a growing circle of Catholic friends and on occasion inviting a visiting abbot to dine with them and celebrate Mass to the small fellowship.

After Ethel died in 1943, Julian — then an insurance magnate, philanthropist, and one of Greensboro's leading citizens — approached the bishop of the Diocese of North Carolina. He wanted to build a substantial house of worship for the people of his wife's faith — in honor of her life and her special devotion to Mary.

Price chose a scaled-down model of the Church of Our Lady of Refuge in Brooklyn, New York, as the model and presented Bishop Vincent Waters of Raleigh with $400,000 in 1946 to get the project under way. Tragically, Price died in an automobile accident that very year and never saw the church even begun. When rising post–World War II building costs delayed construction, the Prices' children, Kathleen Price Bryan and Ralph Price, stepped forward with a $300,000 gift and the church was finally completed in 1952.

The exterior walls are made of North Carolina granite, quarried in Salisbury, with limestone trim from Indiana. The stained-glass windows are made up of 30,000 separate pieces of glass from Belgium. The first Mass was celebrated on July 13, 1952.

The continuing generosity of the Price and Bryan families has enriched Our Lady of Grace through its 50-plus years. In gratitude, the church commissioned a bronze sculpture of the Pieta *(right)* by Edward Fenno Hoffman as a tribute to Kathleen Price Bryan in 1977. The statue stands in a small chapel off the main entrance of the church.

On its 25th anniversary in 1977, the church installed a 2,226-pipe Kleuker organ. Named "Jubilee," it marks both the silver anniversary of the parish and the golden anniversary of Kathleen Bryan and her husband, Joseph. — *Keith McKenzie*

Location: **Greensboro, Guilford County**

Church Completed: **1952**

Worship: **Regular Mass**

The Pageantry of Faith
DORMITION OF THE THEOTOKOS
GREEK ORTHODOX CHURCH

Greensboro's Greek community took shape in the 1930s, formed by immigrant families accustomed to hard times but determined to put down roots and worship according to the traditions of their ancient religion. In time, they gained prosperity and fulfilled their greatest dream, establishment of the Dormition of the Theotokos Greek Orthodox Church.

Dormition of the Theotokos is a vibrant congregation boasting a wide international membership, but it was a long time happening. Until 1946, church members gathered for services on the second floor of a Greek-owned restaurant. In 1948, they moved into a modified two-story house. In 1955, they bought a four-acre site and formed the Hellenic Community Center, a site for recreation and Sunday school. In 1974, they laid the cornerstone on their large church on the corner of Friendly Avenue and Westridge Road, where they remain to this day.

"We came from Greece. We didn't know the language. We didn't have money. We didn't have anything but the willingness to work hard. But we brought you one thing — our religion."
— GUS KATSIKAS, ONE OF THE ORIGINAL MEMBERS OF THE GREEK CHURCH IN GREENSBORO

The exterior of the church *(above)* is white and unadorned, in contrast to the Byzantine décor of the interior and the pageantry of the service. It is a scene of elaborate imagery and impressive energy — the kissing of sacred icons, the procession of a robed priest carrying a large Bible with a gold cover, songs from a choir, readings from the Bible delivered in deep and piercing chants, and all heightened by flickering candles and the exotic scent of incense.

Greeks are now a minority at Dormition of the Theotokos (a name that refers to the "falling asleep of the Mother of God"). The congregation includes Russians, Ukrainians, Serbs, Romanians, Palestinians, and many other nationalities who are both new Americans or long established. The parish is so rich in cultural diversity that the Gospel is read in 16 languages at the Great Easter Service.

The church-sponsored Greek Festival has been a popular autumn tradition in Greensboro since 1983, featuring live music, dancing, Mediterranean delicacies, and guided tours of the church. The festival in recent years has attracted crowds of as many as 10,000 people to enjoy the culture and learn more about the Greek Orthodox religion. — *Keith McKenzie*

Location: **Greensboro, Guilford County**

Current Church Completed: **1974**

Worship: **Regular Services**

THEATER OF THE COSMOS: The Rev. Vasile Mihai stands before the altar — the Holy of Holies — in a luminous shimmer of golden backgrounds. The entire scene serves as a tangible evocation of the celestial order — heaven seems to meet earth in wordless beauty.

Turning the Other Cheek
PLEASANT RIDGE UNITED CHURCH OF CHRIST

Ann Sumner remembers the hot summer night in 1996 when her faith — and the faith of her fellow parishioners — was put through a test of fire.

About 4 a.m., she and her husband were awakened by a frantic knock at the door and cries of "Our church is burning! Our church is burning!" From their yard in northwest Greensboro, a quarter-mile from Pleasant Ridge United Church of Christ, they could see the eerie orange glow against the night sky. Hurrying to the church — where Ann Sumner had been a member her entire life — the couple tearfully watched it go up in flames.

The fire, set by two local teenagers, was easily the darkest chapter in the long history of the church, established in 1867 and in the same location since 1884. But the blaze kindled a spiritual fire within the small congregation, which met and agreed to remain committed to its church home.

The following Sunday, members gathered on the church grounds for an emotional and surreal worship service. The church lay in rubble and ashes, surrounded by crime-scene tape. Members sifted through the debris, finding such remnants as partially burned hymnals and charred Bibles. They brought chairs from the educational building, which had escaped major damage, set them up under the trees, and worshiped.

Although worried about their church's future, members grew determined to make something good of this tragedy. They decided to rebuild where the original church had stood. Within two years, the new church *(right)* was finished and paid for.

Donations and labor came from all over, and members invested their own money and time into the rebuilding. When they gathered to dedicate the church on March 29, 1998, it looked very much like the white, wooden church that had burned. The original metal cross, salvaged from the ruins of the fire, cleaned, and painted, sat atop the steeple.

The Rev. Beth Lilly, who was ordained at Pleasant Ridge in 1985, captured the joyous feelings of the congregation that day. "Take off your shoes," she told the assembly. "Custom is to take off one's shoes when standing on holy ground. This place is, indeed, holy ground."

On that day, the congregation paused to think of the two young men who had caused the destruction. "I think the congregation has forgiven them," the Rev. Paul Davis, then-pastor of the church, told a local reporter. "It's good to remember and learn from it. The chance to forgive is the chance to move on."

And move on the congregation did. The fire and subsequent rebuilding unified the congregation and made it stronger. According to Sumner, the church received about $17,000 in a negotiated settlement from the two young men, and members voted to send the money to two other North Carolina churches that had recently burned.

"It's really wonderful," she said, "to see all the good that came out of something that started out so bad." — *Jimmy Tomlin*

Location: **Greensboro, Guilford County**

Current Church Completed: **1998**

Worship: **Regular Services**

The Churches That Stearns Built

SANDY CREEK CHURCH

Location: **Liberty, Randolph County**

Original Log Church
Completed: **1802**

Worship: *Sandy Creek Baptist:*
Regular Services

Sandy Creek Primitive Baptist:
Third Weekend of the Month

On a rural Randolph County road, passers-by can still gaze at the original Sandy Creek Church, a log building with a profound heritage. The old meetinghouse *(above)* is the birthplace of countless Baptist churches throughout the South.

The story of Sandy Creek begins with one man — Shubal Stearns. Swept up by the fervor of the First Great Awakening, the New England native converted to the New Light movement, whose followers believed God brought "new light" into their hearts through a conversion experience. This reliance on evangelism conflicted with the Old Light rejection of emotionalism, so Stearns and other New Lights founded separate churches, known as "Separates." He became an ordained Separate Baptist minister in 1751; central to his ministry was the doctrine of adult baptism by immersion, rather than the practice of infant baptism or sprinkling.

In 1755 Stearns and his wife arrived in Randolph County accompanied by six other couples and founded Sandy Creek Church. Although small in stature, Stearns was a charismatic speaker whose message resonated with people. By 1758, the church had grown to 606 members; by 1772, a year after Sterns' death, Sandy Creek had become, according to many sources, "mother, grandmother, and great-grandmother" to 42 churches, from which 125 members entered the ministry. By 1775, churches as far north and east as the Potomac River and the Chesapeake Bay, as far south as Georgia, and as far west as the Mississippi River traced their roots to Sandy Creek.

In the mid-1830s, Stearns' church split into Sandy Creek Baptist Church and Sandy Creek Primitive Baptist Church. Some congregants opposed involvement with such institutions as the Baptist State Convention, the Missionary Society, and Sunday school, citing a lack of scriptural support for them. These folks continued to worship in the log building that the church built around 1802 and became Sandy Creek Primitive Baptist. In 1946 they built their current church *(far right)*. Members who favored affiliation with these organizations left the log structure and continued their worship nearby as Sandy Creek Baptist Church *(far left, opposite page)*. Today, each congregation has its own white frame building on either side of the old church, residing peacefully but separately. — *Kathy Grant Westbrook*

Teach Your Children Well
BETHANY UNITED CHURCH OF CHRIST

Location: **Sedalia,
Guilford County**

Church Completed: **1870s**

Worship: **Regular Services**

Many voices have filled Bethany United Church of Christ — those of worshipers and students. Throughout its history, Bethany has been dedicated to Christian education, both for its congregation and in association with Palmer Institute, a private African-American school that for most of the 20th century played a vital role in eastern Guilford County.

In 1870, residents of the community of Sedalia began meeting in the Old Foundry when the American Missionary Association (AMA) sent a minister to educate the area's newly freed slaves. Members soon constructed a simple frame building, adorned with stained-glass windows and topped with a short steeple. That building today wears a sandy brick veneer.

On Sunday mornings the church filled with worshipers, but it received its heaviest use during the week when school was held for area children. Girls slept in the church attic while boys lived at the parish house.

In 1901, the AMA sent Dr. Charlotte Hawkins Brown to teach at the school, which was then called Bethany Institute. A year later the school closed its doors, but Brown stayed and opened Palmer Institute across the road. As her school grew, so did the participation of students at Bethany Church, where Brown became a leading member. Before long, the number of students attending the church exceeded those from the community.

Brown insisted that services be formal. "The services were conducted in a quiet and sophisticated manner," said Ruth Totton *(right)*, a member of the church and former teacher and administrator at Palmer. "If a minister used bad grammar during a sermon, Miss Brown would be sure and bring it to his attention before the next week."

As time passed, the number of Palmer students attending Bethany dwindled. Then, in 1952, Brown became ill and stepped down as the school's president.

But her legacy lives on. "Our church was started by a missionary and we are a missionary church," said Totton. "We are here for the people of Sedalia, and the same bell rings every Sunday morning as it has for years."

It echoes across U.S. Highway 70 to where one woman transformed countless young lives and to the future of a congregation that still reaches out to and enriches its community. — *Diane Silcox-Jarrett*

"I Have Called You Friends" — *John 15:14*
DEEP RIVER FRIENDS MEETING

History knows the name of Deep River Friends, who began worshiping in the wilderness of the Deep River area in what is now northern High Point in 1754. They built their first meetinghouse in 1758.

In the 1750s, migrating Quakers from Pennsylvania began settling in Guilford County. In addition to Deep River, they established societies at Jamestown and New Garden. Jamestown's meetinghouse, restored and on exhibit at Mendenhall Plantation, is the oldest in the state. New Garden began meeting in 1751 and established Guilford College, the first coeducational institution in the South.

The Society of Friends has a long history of supporting equal rights for all races and genders, and evidence of that basic tenet turns up often in the history of Deep River. In the 19th century, church members are believed to have participated in the Underground Railroad, the network of sympathetic white Americans who helped slaves in the South escape to the North before the Civil War. Members have also played an active role in the civil-rights movement and efforts to stop the war in Vietnam.

Deep River also has a history of extending equal rights to women. According to Florence Allen, a member of Deep River for nearly 80 years and its unofficial historian, "Quakers allowed women to preach long before other denominations did." The first paid minister of Deep River Friends was Bessie Field, who came to the church in 1916.

For many years, Friends did not employ full-time pastors. "There were traveling ministers who would come through the area, stay a few weeks and then move on," Allen said. "That's the way it was at our church until 1916, when Bessie Field came."

In contemporary times, Deep River Friends no longer finds itself surrounded by wilderness but by urban development. The meetinghouse sits at one of the county's busiest intersections. Although offers for their coveted property have been lucrative, members have refused to sell. "We like to think we're pretty well-grounded here," said Allen. The church and developers are not the only ones who recognize the church's historical significance. In 1996, the meetinghouse and the cemetery were listed on the National Register of Historic Places. — *Jimmy Tomlin*

Location: **High Point, Guilford County**

Current Church Completed: **1875**

Worship: **Regular Services**

Golden Glory
FIRST BAPTIST CHURCH

The monumental First Baptist Church in Winston-Salem dates its birth to a meeting of just five people of the faith in 1871. The town was on the verge of the tobacco era. Richard Joshua Reynolds started a tobacco factory in 1875, and both the town and church greatly expanded during the boom created by R.J. Reynolds Tobacco Co.

That original fellowship of Baptists organized by Alfred Holland created the nucleus of a congregation. By 1877 the first church building was built, and two years later the church was self-supporting. A second church was constructed in 1893, and a third building followed in 1901.

From 1893 until 1917, the Baptist congregation made an indelible impression and had a major influence on the entire area. The church's Dr. H.A. Brown was the catalyst. An exceptional preacher and leader, he created a mission strategy for the formation of Baptist churches on every quadrant in the town. During his charge, First Baptist grew to 535 members, sponsored three additional Baptist congregations, and helped with the organization of many more. Another legacy of his leadership was the raising of $100,000 to bring Baptist Hospital to Winston-Salem.

The 1920s saw material advance on a scale and pace unprecedented for Winston-Salem. At First Baptist, several businessmen initiated a drive to build yet another church — this one massive in size and magnificent in design that would be unmatched in the city, a testament to the church's dynamic growth and faith. In 1925, as First Baptist moved into its new home, the congregation was the largest in the city with 2,000 members.

A mix of architectural styles, the domed church brings to mind the circular templates of Rome. The ornamentation is elaborate and essentially from Greek influences. Corinthian columns stand 24 feet tall and encircle the auditorium. The dome ceiling floats some 60 feet above the congregation. The three-stage steeple reaches 155 feet above the sidewalk.

Even so, the point that this is a Baptist church is not lost. The baptistery stands aloft, a focal spot of beauty visible from any point in the auditorium.
— *Keith McKenzie*

Location: **Winston-Salem, Forsyth County**

Current Church Completed: **1925**

Worship: **Regular Services**

Higher Education
WAIT CHAPEL

Location: **Wake Forest University, Winston-Salem, Forsyth County**

Current Church Completed: **1956**

Worship: **Regular Services**

At Wake Forest University, the influence of Wait Chapel, named for the college's first president, has been nothing short of angelic since its construction as a nucleus of the esteemed Baptist college in Winston-Salem. Dedicated on October 12-13, 1956, the 2,100-seat chapel has been host to worship services, compulsory chapel meetings (which ended in 1969), distinguished lecturers and musicians, and presidential debates.

Structurally, Wait Chapel is magnificent, from its old Virginia, Jefferson-style brick exterior to its majestic stucco columns and copper roof and steeple. The sanctuary is complemented by a grand, four-manual pipe organ with 3,696 pipes.

With grace and grandeur, Wait Chapel continues to serve as a sacred house of worship. Wake Forest Baptist Church, which was organized in the town of Wake Forest just before the school's move to Winston-Salem, still worships in Wait Chapel every Sunday morning. And every December, the chapel holds a traditional Moravian lovefeast *(above)* that is believed to be the largest indoor service of a lovefeast in North America. — *Jimmy Tomlin*

A Place to Call Home
HOME MORAVIAN CHURCH

Location: **Old Salem, Winston-Salem, Forsyth County**

Church Completed: **1800**

Worship: **Regular Services**

The Moravians, a devout mission-focused fellowship that traces its beginnings to central Europe in the Middle Ages, began immigrating to America in the early 1700s and branched out to the South after first establishing successful communities in Pennsylvania.

Shortly after mid-century, the hardy religious pioneers were building footholds on the huge tract of North Carolina wilderness they named Wachovia — land that comprises half of modern-day Forsyth County. Although those vast church holdings are gone now, the denomination sustains its Wachovia legacy through two-dozen active congregations in Winston-Salem alone. In the restored historic village of Old Salem, the denomination's Southern headquarters, Home Moravian Church still calls the brethren to worship each Sunday as it has since 1800.

The Salem congregation got its start in the winter of 1766, when a small band of skilled Moravian builders from the Bethabara and Bethania settlements traveled several miles south with a wagonload of tools and supplies to begin creating a central trading town. Space for worship services was among the first priorities. A floor of the second house they completed served this purpose until a separate Gemein Saal (congregation hall) could be built in 1771.

In 1798, construction began on the simple brick church that anchors a corner of the town square and which today ministers to the largest Moravian congregation in the country. The church has been in continuous operation since opening, except during several periods of renovations. One of those times was in 1910, when the historic Tannenberg pipe organ, which had been in the church since its opening day, was removed.

Most of the pieces of the old Tannenberg, built by America's first professional organ manufacturer and his largest surviving instrument, were found in storage and put back together in an extraordinary restoration that culminated in 2004 with its unveiling in a new auditorium at the Old Salem visitor center. The magnificent organ (above) is on permanent loan there courtesy of Home Moravian Church.

Visitors to Home Moravian for its yuletide lovefeast service may not hear the Tannenberg but they are welcomed to partake in a cherished church tradition — the sharing of sweet buns and mugs of coffee, the lighting of handmade beeswax candles, the simple decorations of evergreen garlands, and the carols of the choir. — *Keith McKenzie*

Liberty for All

ST. PHILIPS MORAVIAN CHURCH

From Salem's initial settlement in 1766, African-Americans — both free and slave — have played an enduring role in the community's moral and social fiber. In the early phases, they were received as members of the village and the church. They helped build the town and participated in its commerce.

After the segregation of Salem's Moravian church in 1822, black brethren received their own mission, which today remains the oldest African-American Moravian congregation in the United States. On December 23, 1823, their log church *(building to the far left in photograph)* at the southern end of Salem was consecrated amid much festivity, with dignitaries, a church band, and about 90 African-Americans attending.

For decades, black worshipers from a nearby area known as Happy Hill would trek across Salem Creek for services; soon the church became a focal point of Winston-Salem's African-American community.

For almost 40 years, the congregation met here. In the late 1850s, a larger brick church building *(far right)* went up adjacent to the original church and graveyard and was consecrated in December 1861.

The day of freedom for St. Philips members came on May 21, 1865. As they crowded into their new church, spacious and filled with light, a Union officer marched down the aisle. The Rev. Seth G. Clark of the 10th Ohio Cavalry read from the book of First Corinthians and announced Emancipation. Upon hearing the news, the congregation began to sing.

Bishop Edward Rondthaler gave the brick church the name St. Philips in December 1914. In 1952, the congregation moved to the Happy Hill neighborhood and a chapel was built there in 1959. The church moved again in 1967 because of highway construction, this time to Bon Air Avenue, where it continues to serve the neighborhood.

In Salem, the church's roots are not forgotten. The 1823 log church has been rebuilt, and the oldest slave church standing in the state — the 1861 brick structure — has also undergone restoration.

With the end of slavery, many members left St. Philips, but a core remained. Longtime member Melvin Oats conveyed a reason. "Tradition kept us here; the desire for more excitement was a continual pull." — *Keith McKenzie*

Location: **Old Salem, Winston-Salem, Forsyth County**

Brick Church Completed: **1861**

Worship: *Brick Church:* **Restored and Open to the Public**
Log Church: **Reconstructed and Houses Exhibits**

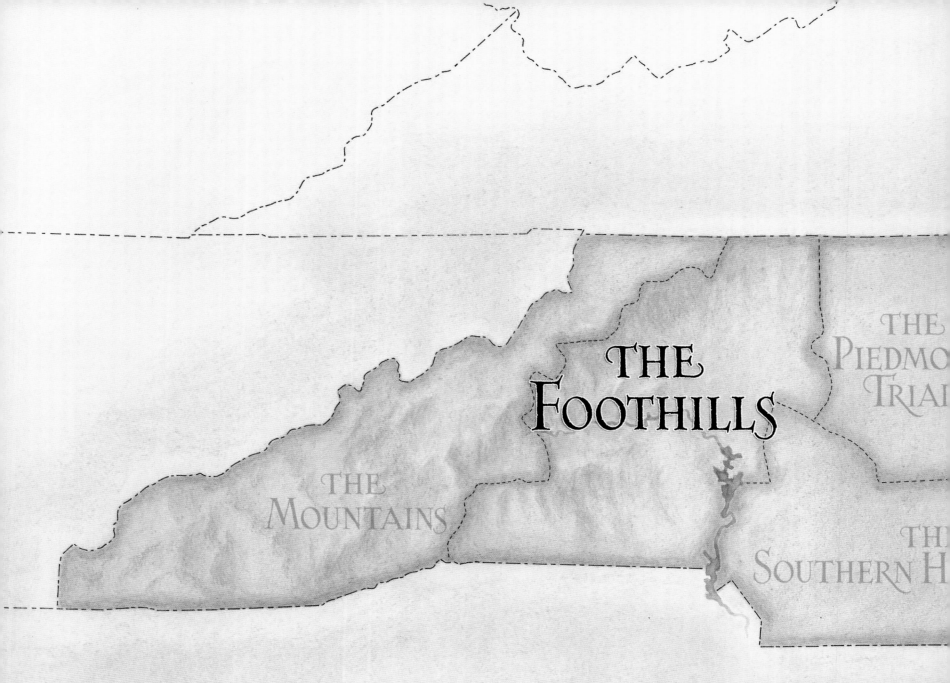

THE
FOOTHILLS

THE
MOUNTAINS

THE
PIEDMO
TRIA

THE
SOUTHERN H

CHAPTER SIX

"Be Not Conformed to this World"
— *Romans 12:2*
UNION GROVE AMISH CHURCH

In a rural community straddling the Iredell and Yadkin county lines, there stands a simple white frame meetinghouse — no lofty bell tower, no stained-glass windows. In the church's grassy "parking lot," there are no cars — only a row of horse-drawn buggies.

Welcome to Union Grove Amish Church, North Carolina's only true Amish community house of worship. Steeped in traditions from the German Reformation, the Amish meet here on Sunday mornings, encouraging humility and community while rejecting worldly influences. According to Mark Schlabach, the presiding bishop of the church, the Amish "believe in a total separation from the world, that we're not to be following the fads and fashions of the world. That's why we refrain from TV, radio, computer, internet — we see that as assimilation with the world."

Men and women enter the church through separate doors at opposite ends of the building and sit on opposite sides of the church. "The symbolism of that," explained church member Tom Coletti, "is that we see the whole congregation as a family, so we don't sit as individual families."

In addition, services are conducted entirely in German, a distinct nod to the roots of the Amish faith. "This is the language the forefathers brought over from Germany, and the Amish have chosen to retain the language," Coletti said. "We use Martin Luther's translation of the Bible. Preaching is in the Pennsylvania German dialect, and scriptures, prayers, and hymns are all in High German."

Schlabach, a seventh-generation Amish, added that worshiping in German is also a reflection of their desire to honor the scriptural decree to "be not conformed to this world." (Romans 12:2)

At Union Grove, the bishop performs the sacraments and two ministers preside over worship services, which typically consist of a short opening sermon and a second sermon that's usually an hour or longer. Sandwiched around the sermons are German prayers, New Testament readings, individual testimonies, and hymns — which are sung a cappella.

The Amish settled in North Carolina's foothills in 1985, drawn here by the climate, fertile farmlands, and state laws that let them operate a private school. The church, built in 1990, now has about 110 adult members, representing about 20 households. — *Jimmy Tomlin*

Location: **Hamptonville, Yadkin County**

Church Completed: **1990**

Worship: **Regular Services**

THE SIMPLE LIFE: The Amish know they stand out but are comfortable with their way of life — and have no plans to change. "It's all about not conforming to this world," Mark Schlabach said. "Once we start assimilating with the world, the easier it is to be swept in with the tide of the world and what the world has to offer."

I Love to Tell the Story
GRACE MORAVIAN CHURCH

Mount Airy's Moravian community began taking root as early travelers stopped to rest along the Great Wagon Road from the North in the 1700s and gained momentum as members of the faith from other outposts — including Salem to the south — settled in. Their simple church on Main Street dates to 1925, one of the first buildings in town built from Mount Airy's famous native granite.

The establishment of the church came through the influence and tireless efforts of the Rev. Charles Crouch. After preaching to an assembly of about 60 people at the Mount Airy town hall in 1923, he remarked that "some of the people are moving for a church lot in Mount Airy and regular preaching, which we hope to give them from now on." The congregation held its first service in a store building in 1924. According to the *Wachovia Moravian*, the faith's monthly newspaper, "Ninety-six were baptized and the church received the largest number to be added at one time and at one place in our history."

The church graveyard, known as "God's Acre," is plain, symmetrical, and ordered, its rows of flat granite gravestones arranged by fellowships, which Moravians call "choirs." In the Moravian church, choir refers to a group of people who are at the same station in life. Men, women, and children are all buried in their choirs, not with their biological families — symbolic of the spiritual unity of the family of God.

Part of the church's unique North Carolina lore involves Mount Airy's most famous native son, Andy Griffith *(dressed in coat and tie, right)*. Although he spent his childhood in Haymore Baptist Church, Andy grew close ties with Grace Moravian because he wanted to learn to play the trombone and the Rev. Ed Mickey offered the only music lessons in town. He sang in the choir and played in the brass band at Grace and also traveled locally with the pastor to provide music and worship service to other churches and groups. Mickey's brass, wind, and guitar instruction and mentoring certainly paid off. Among his many lifetime achievements, Andy won a Grammy Award in 1997 for his collection of gospel hymns, *I Love to Tell the Story*. — *Keith McKenzie*

Location: **Mount Airy, Surry County**

Church Completed: **1925**

Worship: **Regular Services**

Pilgrimages
ST. PAUL'S EPISCOPAL CHURCH

Location: **Wilkesboro,
Wilkes County**

Church Completed: **1849**

Worship: **Regular Services**

One of only a few Gothic Revival churches built in western North Carolina before the Civil War, St. Paul's Episcopal Church reflects the influence of the "high church" Ecclesiological Movement that emphasized ritual and religious decoration. Consecrated in 1849, the compact brick church is largely unchanged today, though complemented in 1990 with the construction of a new sanctuary. A corridor linking the old with the new features two frescoes by famed North Carolina artist Ben Long: *The Imprisonment of St. Paul* and *The Enlightenment of St. Paul*.

The church was designed by its rector, William Gries, who had studied at the Valle Crucis Seminary established by Bishop Levi Silliman Ives. The Wilkesboro church traces its beginnings to Ives' baptism of three children in the town in 1836. For the dedication of St. Paul's, a delegation from the seminary walked 45 miles to Wilkesboro and marched into the town wearing the vestments of the church.

The wooded grounds of St. Paul's include a graveyard and the contemplative outdoor setting of Coventry Chapel, encircled by a broken wall of stone. It's a symbol of renewal and hope styled after St. Michael's Cathedral in Coventry, England, a 14th-century church mostly demolished by a German bombing raid in World War II, but which now provides entry to a new cathedral built beside the ruins. In Wilkesboro, St. Paul's "ruined" wall provides access to its new sanctuary. In a distinct adaptation of a medieval practice, Coventry Chapel also includes a replica of the labyrinth at Chartres Cathedral in France. The redbrick walk *(right)* represents the pilgrimage to the Holy Land required by the Church in the Middle Ages. — *Keith McKenzie*

Come to the Church in the Wildwood
MARIAH'S CHAPEL

Location: **Grandin, Caldwell County**

Church Completed: **1879**

Worship: **Regular Services**

Atop high ground overlooking the Yadkin River in the hamlet of Grandin, the brilliant white frame church known as Mariah's Chapel was built in 1879 as a community house of worship in Happy Valley near Lenoir — open to all of Christian faith but particularly serving Methodist and Episcopalian congregations who held their services on alternate Sundays.

The little rectangular building with a belfry above the front gable, sash windows along the sides, and two front doors (separate entrances for men and women) recalls the simple architecture of country churches in the 19th century. The sanctuary was designed for sharing. The half-circled chancel suited the needs of Methodists who approached front and center for prayers and also those of Episcopalians who came to receive Holy Communion.

Martha Maria Earnest donated two acres of land in 1878 "in consideration of a sense of duty to the church of God" and held worship services in her home nearby until the chapel could be built. It is generally accepted that the chapel is named for her, despite the variation in the spelling of the two names. A second theory, however, speculates that the name is a variation of biblical Mount Moriah.

In its early years, the church invited residents from throughout Caldwell County to "singing schools" in spring and summer. The schools were devoted to the rudiments of note reading and sight singing, with a focus on sacred music. Instruction was a cappella — the church had no organ at the time. The congregations of Mariah's Chapel also ministered to the community through a mission that distributed food to the needy and toys to the children of poor farmers. — *Keith McKenzie*

Coming to America
WALDENSIAN PRESBYTERIAN CHURCH

It was the end of an incredible journey in the spring of 1893 when the Waldenses, a persecuted group of Protestants from the Italian Alps, stepped off a train in the Burke County community of Valdese.

Today, descendants of those determined immigrants still make up the majority of the membership of the Waldensian Presbyterian Church their families founded. "About 65 percent of the church members are direct ancestors," said Francis Tron, a volunteer at the Waldensian Museum, which is owned by the church. "We're a stubborn group of people."

Indeed, Waldenses have had to be. For hundreds of years members of the tiny evangelical sect in the Cottian Alps of northwest Italy were persecuted by the French and Italian governments because they did not conform to the laws of the Roman Catholic Church. Years of oppression and overpopulation aroused in these stoic people a desire for a better life. When American landowner Marvin Scaife heard of the Waldenses' interest in coming to America, he sold the group a tract of land near the Catawba River.

Two scouts were sent to survey the land. They came back with a positive report, and the first detachment of 29 arrived on May 29, 1893. The Rev. Charles Albert Tron wrote of that historic moment, "The arrival produced a profound emotion … [and they] did not hesitate to bend their knees in thanks to God and invoke His favor for the newborn colony. To see all the bared heads and the weeping women and children was a scene which cannot be forgotten."

Soon after arriving, the Waldenses began planning their church — a massive, stuccoed building in the heart of the village. Completed in 1899, the church evokes a European feel with its slate roof, courtyards, fountain, and stone walls *(right)*.

The Waldenses chose their adopted country's day of independence on which to dedicate their beloved church. On July 4, 1899, the proud new citizens borrowed an American flag to wave over the ceremonies. Not knowing how to hang it, they innocently hung the flag upside down. — *Deena C. Bouknight*

Location: **Valdese, Burke County**

Church Completed: **1899**

Worship: **Regular Services**

"Let the Little Children Come to Me" — *Matthew 19:14*
CONCORDIA LUTHERAN CHURCH

A brown bag full of nuts, candy, and fruit — that is something I will always remember," recalled Shirley Conrobert, a lifetime member of Concordia Lutheran Church. "Every year after the children's Christmas pageant the grownups would hand out these bags of goodies for us."

For many years the children of Concordia have known this simple gesture as part of their Christmas. Tradition and children have been important parts of Concordia Lutheran Church for more than 125 years.

In 1877, Lutheran congregations in Catawba County established a high school, which was to be of "strictly Lutheran character." The school operated as an academy until 1883 when it became Concordia College, principally to prepare young men for the ministry. At first worship services were held in the assembly hall; but as the college grew, the need for a church became greater. Concordia's first church was built in the early 1890s.

In 1894 the church took over grades one through seven from the college and opened what is today Concordia Christian Day School. Although Concordia College closed in 1935 after a fire, the day school continues to thrive.

The church, too, flourished, and as a result of its growth, a new sanctuary was built in 1958. Designed by Charlotte architect A.G. Odell, the building exemplifies bold modernist architecture with its geometric composition, broad roof, and jewel-tone stained glass *(right)*.

The bold design drew enormous attention; the church was dedicated in February and by May 18 more than 6,000 people had visited it. The *Hickory Daily Record* wrote, "There is no other like it in the United States or probably anywhere else."

The open space where the original church building had stood now serves as playing fields for the school — not surprising for a congregation devoted to Lutheran education and making sure each Christmas there are brown paper bags full of nuts, fruits, and candy for its children. — *Diane Silcox-Jarrett*

ROCK SPRINGS
CAMP MEETING GROUND
ON AUGUST 7, 1830, FORTY ACRES OF LAND WERE DEED
ROCK SPRINGS CAMP GROUND TRUSTEES FOR USE BY TH
METHODIST CHURCH. LATER LOTS WERE LAID OUT AND
THE ARBOR WAS CONSTRUCTED IN 1832 WHICH PREDATED
ENTERED IN THE NATIONAL REGISTER OF HISTORIC
SEPT. 22, 1972, ROCK SPRINGS CAMP MEETING GRO
FIRST IN NORTH CAROLINA AND POSSIBLY THE
COUNTRY. CAMP MEETING OCCURS DURING THE
AUGUST EACH YEAR.
BECAUSE OF HER LOVE AND DEDICATION
CAMP MEETING GROUND. THIS MONUMENT
LOVING MEMORY OF GEORGIANNA HOWAR
FAMILY AND FRIENDS

That Old-Time Religion
ROCK SPRINGS CAMP MEETING GROUND
TUCKER'S GROVE CAMP MEETING GROUND

Rock Springs Camp Meeting, one of the oldest and most celebrated of North Carolina's religious revival events, sprang from the powerful evangelical phenomenon known as the "Second Great Awakening" that swept across the Protestant landscape in America from the 1790s to the 1840s.

The Rock Springs meeting traces its roots to 1794, when Daniel Asbury, a famous circuit-riding Methodist minister from Virginia, arrived in the Denver area to establish the tradition. The meeting moved to its current 45-acre home in 1830, gaining its name from the two springs on the site and the large numbers of rocks. The meeting is still going strong today, a cherished event for thousands of families who come together for a week of faith and fellowship each August.

The first camp meetings in North Carolina were held in woods, with families sleeping in their wagons or on the ground and cooking over campfires. The Rock Springs campground, though rustic, is laid out in the style of a town — and in fact has been incorporated since 1851. About 258 roughly built, dirt-floor cabins — called "tents" — are arrayed around the "arbor," a roofed, open-sided meeting pavilion large enough to shelter a thousand people. The tents are individually owned, passed down from one generation to the next.

The camp setting has traditionally encouraged worshipers to openly proclaim their spiritual emotions through rhapsodic shouting, clapping, hugging, kissing, and laughing — a vibrant form of piety that has not always been deemed acceptable within the walls of their churches back home. Samuel McCorkle, the illustrious 19th-century Presbyterian minister, attended a camp meeting in hopes of understanding why so many members of his faith were drawn to it. He is said to have left "baffled beyond description."

A few miles from Rock Springs is Tucker's Grove Camp Meeting Ground, one of the oldest continuous black meetings in the South. Smaller in size, it includes 102 tents. Brevard Chapel was built in the 1870s as a church for black members of the Rock Springs and Tucker's Grove camp meetings. The timber for the little white church came from the Rock Springs site. Affiliated with the United Methodist Church, the chapel still holds regular Sunday services. — *Keith McKenzie*

**Rock Springs
Camp Meeting Ground**
Location: **Denver, Lincoln County**
Organized: **1830**
Worship: **Annual Revival
in August**

**Tucker's Grove
Camp Meeting Ground**
Location: **Machpelah,
Lincoln County**
Organized: **1871**
Worship: **Annual Revival
in August**

SHALL WE GATHER: Though organized by Methodists, the Rock Springs community encompasses a broad spectrum of Protestant faiths and peoples *(right)*. At Tucker's Grove Camp Meeting *(below)* the open arbor comes alive each August, with fellowship, food, and nightly worship services. Since 1876, it has been operated by nearby Brevard Chapel *(below right)*.

Following the Rule of St. Benedict
ABBEY BASILICA OF MARYHELP OF CHRISTIANS

Location: **Belmont, Gaston County**

Current Church Completed: **1893**

Worship: **Regular Services**

The abbey basilica, college, and monastery collectively called Belmont Abbey began in 1870 when Jeremiah O'Connell, a circuit-riding Catholic priest bought a 500-acre farm near the Catawba River and promptly gave it to the Benedictine monks of St. Vincent's Archabbey in Pennsylvania.

Six years later, Herman Wolfe arrived from St. Vincent's to begin a Benedictine monastery, the first in the Southeast. With only two students accompanying him, Wolfe was given the task to "serve as a professor, establish a monastic farm, and be a Catholic priest to a town thought to have no Catholics." The fledgling group built a wooden chapel, but used the area's abundant red clay to construct a college building.

In 1884, Wolfe's abbey gained independent status, confirmed by Pope Leo XIII, and was given the name of Maryhelp Abbey. The monastery's highly respected college, now called Belmont Abbey College, was chartered in 1886.

In 1892 construction of the Abbey Basilica of Maryhelp of Christians began, and the first Mass was celebrated within its magnificent walls the following year. Designated a minor basilica by Pope Paul II in 1998, the church is also constructed of red clay, stone, and wood. The monks supplied much of the labor, thus keeping construction costs to a mere $60,000. In 1909, a clock *(right)* was added to one of its two spired towers. From the 150-foot west tower tolls three bells, the largest of which — named Saint Mary — weighs 1,500 pounds.

The baptismal font in the narthex is said to be an American Indian altar once used as a slave auction block *(above)*. A brass plate on the font tells of its past and present: "Upon this rock, men once were sold into slavery. Now upon this rock, through the waters of Baptism, men become free children of God." It is a simple piece full of history — a piece that represents how the monks at Belmont Abbey live simply alongside history. — *Diane Silcox-Jarrett*

"Love Thy Neighbour" — *Matthew 22:39*
CHURCH OF THE GOOD SHEPHERD

Each Sunday the religious and social profundity of Church of the Good Shepherd can be seen on the faces of its parishioners, both black and white.

Now safely tucked in Tryon, the white frame church was built in 1906, very likely by ex-slaves and their descendants on the Green River Plantation in rural Polk County. Mary Coxe, widow of the plantation's post-Civil War owner, donated the funds for the church. Called St. Andrews, the church held regular services until after World War I, when attendance gradually declined and the property was abandoned.

In the meantime, in Tryon, the Tryon Industrial Colored School was built in the early 1900s to educate African-Americans. By 1907, more than 100 students gained instruction, and they also held regular worship services. This school was the beginning of the mission of Good Shepherd.

As public education for black students improved, the school was no longer needed and fell into disrepair — even though worship services were still held. By the 1940s, the small congregation of Good Shepherd that had been meeting at the school needed a church in which to worship and knew that the church at Green River had been abandoned.

As Jewel Booker Green, a student at the school and longtime church member said, "St. Andrews had a building, but no members, and Good Shepherd had members but no building."

So in 1955, the chapel on Green River Plantation about 40 miles away was carefully moved in four sections to the site of the old industrial school in Tryon and reassembled.

Before Good Shepherd acquired its building, black priests led the services. After 1955, for no apparent reason the priests have all been white — at least until recently. In 2003, the Rev. Walter Bryan, an African-American who grew up attending services at Good Shepherd, returned to Tryon as its pastor.

Also since 1955, many white people have visited Good Shepherd and often stayed. Today the small congregation is comprised equally of black and white members. — *Deena C. Bouknight*

Location: **Tryon,
Polk County**

Moved to Current Location:
1955

Worship: **Regular Services**

Southern Honor
EPISCOPAL CHURCH
OF ST. JOHN IN THE WILDERNESS

Military heroes and business magnates are buried among the towering pines and hemlocks in the graveyard of the Episcopal Church of St. John in the Wilderness. Many were members of antebellum Southern aristocratic families who spent their summers in this resort area often referred to as the "Little Charleston of the Mountains."

Significant among them were Susan and Charles Baring, originally of the Baring banking firm in London, England. They arrived in 1827 to build their retreat, Mountain Lodge, where Susan could regain her health. Although treading deeply in Baptist territory, the Episcopalian couple immediately began construction of a private estate chapel. When the first building burned, another one followed. In 1836, 20 members of the summer colony formed a congregation and the Barings deeded the church to the Diocese of North Carolina.

As more Lowcountry families flocked to the area, word of the Barings' church spread and St. John became the house of worship and focal point for summer inhabitants. Expanded in 1852, the lovely tan brick chapel features round-arched windows and a sturdy corner tower. Dark stone walls blanketed with damp moss and elaborate iron gates give St. John in the Wilderness a medieval presence.

The church is the resting place of such notable figures as Christopher Gustavus Memminger, first secretary of the Confederate Treasury and builder of "Rock Hill," which later became the home of Carl Sandburg. (Although Sandburg was not a member of the church, his widely attended memorial service was held at St. John in 1967.) Also buried here are members of the families of three signers of the Declaration of Independence.

And of course, the Barings rest here as well. Longtime Flat Rock resident and church member Louise Howe Bailey wrote in a published history of St. John: "Underneath the three pews originally held by the Barings, in the space reserved by them for their burial site, lie the earthly remains of those two people whose devotion to the Episcopal form of worship led them to establish their church within a pioneer settlement where, not many years earlier, the Cherokee Nation had claimed hunting grounds." — *Deena C. Bouknight*

Location: **Flat Rock, Henderson County**

Current Church Completed: **1836**

Worship: **Regular Services**

THE
MOUNTAINS

THE
FOOTHILLS

THE
PIEDMO
TRIA

THE
SOUTHERN H

CHAPTER
SEVEN

THE
TRIANGLE

THE
COASTAL
PLAIN

THE
COAST

ARTLAND

Solid as a Rock
ENGLISH CHAPEL UNITED METHODIST CHURCH

Location: **Pisgah National Forest, Transylvania County**

Current Church Completed: **1940**

Worship: **Regular Services**

Jenny McGaha leads a congregation of about 60 members one fine spring morning in the singing of "Sweet, Sweet Spirit" that professes: "There's a sweet, sweet spirit in this place, and I know that it's the spirit of the Lord."

McGaha is a great-granddaughter of the Rev. A.F. English, founder of English Chapel in 1860 in what is now Pisgah National Forest near Brevard. English, a circuit-riding Methodist minister in western North Carolina before the Civil War, settled in Transylvania County, bought a tract of land from his father-in-law, donated lumber from his own sawmill, and pitched in with neighbors to build a wooden church. Soon, the church also served as a school and a community center.

Change came to the congregation, however, in 1895 when industrialist George Vanderbilt bought about 100,000 acres west of his Biltmore Estate, including Mount Pisgah, to develop Pisgah Forest for commercial use and as a private hunting preserve. He also claimed English Chapel and its school — valued in 1905 at $50 — as part of his holdings. After Vanderbilt's death in 1914, the U.S. government bought the land as one of the first tracts of Pisgah National Forest. Consequently, families living in the area were moved.

But the small chapel maintained its autonomy, and the "sweet spirit" of this rock-solid church is still generated by McGaha and other descendants of English, as well as those whose parents pulled stones out of nearby Davidson River in 1940 to construct the current structure and spell out the name of the church above its doorway *(right)*.

In the early 1990s, English Chapel gained its first full-time Methodist preacher. Although there is a faithful flock every Sunday, the forest's campground and hiking trails also bring in visitors from around the world. — *Deena C. Bouknight*

"Blessed Are the Pure in Heart, for They Shall See God" — *Matthew 5:8*
CHURCH OF THE GOOD SHEPHERD

Location: **Cashiers, Jackson County**

Current Church Completed: **1895**

Worship: **Regular Services**

Church of the Good Shepherd in Cashiers is famous for the steadfastness of its parishioners. Organized in the 1880s by Episcopal missionary John Deal, the remote church in the southwestern pocket of North Carolina primarily served wealthy Episcopalians who spent their summers in the lush Cashiers Valley. But in August 1892, fire destroyed the young mission church, and only the Bible and baptismal font were saved. Undaunted by their loss, members immediately began rebuilding. Charred timbers from the original structure were used in the new church, which was dedicated on September 2, 1895.

Evidence of even more arduous times can be found in the church graveyard. The Grimshawes were an active church family who moved to nearby Whiteside Cove in 1880. When diphtheria struck the region, the father was away, the church was closed for the winter, and no doctor was available. The couple's four daughters — ages two, four, six, and seven — all died within a period of 34 days. In her husband's absence, Mrs. Grimshawe built caskets, dug the graves, buried her children, and read burial passages from the Book of Common Prayer over them. Their graves are marked and protected by a wrought-iron fence *(right)*.

The church itself suffered in the early 20th century when many of its supporters died and financial contributions languished. The church closed its doors, and the weatherboard building fell into ruin.

The fate of the church changed, however, in the 1920s when a group set about saving it and guests of nearby High Hampton Inn began to think of the church as their spiritual home. The church gradually became strong again. On December 2, 1979, it held its first winter service. Today, the church has a full-time priest and a body of year-round and summer members. — *Deena C. Bouknight*

Editor's Note: Church of the Good Shepherd holds special meaning for writer Deena C. Bouknight. The memorial service for her mother, Meta C. Boswell, was held here in August 1991.

Blest Be the Tie That Binds

GILLESPIE CHAPEL

Location: **Cartoogechaye, Macon County**

Church Completed: **1880s**

Worship: **Now a Community Center, Still Open for Special Services and Annual Homecoming**

Like the smoothed mountains that surround it, Gillespie Chapel has been softened by time. Standing stoically in the rural extension of Franklin known as Cartoogechaye, the one-room church is still equipped with oil lamps even though electricity came to the area in the mid-1940s. A pot-bellied stove serves as the only source of heat; plain wooden pews reach across the simply furnished interior. A paint-by-the-number version of *The Last Supper* over the altar is its only adornment. A cemetery spreads out on the steep ascent behind the wood-frame, cedar shake structure.

Like the mountainside on which it rests, the modest church is no stranger to resilience. Built in the 1880s by Franklin architect Zebulon Conley, the chapel served as a school for its first five years. About 1886, Methodists bought the building. The church acquired its name from its first minister, the Rev. John Gillespie. To transform the building from a schoolhouse to a house of worship, an octagonal bell tower was added to the façade. For all the church's simplicity, the bell tower serves as an element of ornate distinction.

For years Gillespie Chapel faithfully served the spiritual needs of its rural mountain congregation, but as years passed it began showing signs of age. Regular services ceased in 1975, although the church still opened its doors for weddings, funerals, and other functions.

In 1986, the chapel was deeded to the Upper Cartoogechaye Community Club, which began using it as a community center. With the Bible left in place, the leader of the club conducts meetings from the pulpit.

The club immediately began planning the chapel's restoration. According to longtime member Edith Byrd, "We raffled off a quilt and made $1,600. We've done two cookbooks and had to get second printings on both. And someone etched an 11-by-14 painting of the church ... we've sold hundreds of those. And we got some grants. Those who gave $100 or more or gave their time for labor, we put their name on a plaque that hangs on the wall in the church." — *Deena C. Bouknight*

A Light Upon the Mountains
FIRST PRESBYTERIAN CHURCH

Location: **Waynesville, Haywood County**

Current Church Completed: **1907**

Worship: **Regular Services**

Pure faith spills over the pews and fills the sanctuary of First Presbyterian Church, nestled on the crest of a hillside corner lot in downtown Waynesville. Music flows from the Rodgers 940 electronic organ, complemented by pipes and a violin in the tiny hands of five-year-old Katelyn Hammel. While this particular Sunday is an especially joyous one — it's young Rev. Joshua Cole's first day in the pulpit — exuberance and exaltation have characterized this creatively designed tan brick church for close to a century.

The church's first full-time pastor, Charles Argyle Campbell, arrived in 1906. According to church history, the Scot was a "brilliant sermonizer and orator — employing his brogue while reading Robert Burns and singing Scotch songs at church socials."

Campbell encouraged socials; in fact, it was during his pastorate that the church's annual Roll Call Dinner began. While food was being served, someone called the roll. It is said that the roll caller liked to "make a pun or purposefully mispronounce a name to add to the fun."

Cole plans to continue the same spirit of joy that has continued through the ages. "My desire is for this church on the corner to be a light that shines for Christ … where people are fed by the gospel."

To help lead the way, lively music reverberates down Main Street on Sundays. At some point, the church installed an electronic bell amplifier so its chimes can be heard a mile away. "I used to think you should go and sit in church in a reverent mood," said church historian Ruby Daniel, "but I decided I was wrong. I love our praise music. I think it brings more celebratory feelings into the church."

Over the years the preachers have matched the fever pitch of the music. First Presbyterian's most famous presence was Calvin Thielman, who preached here in the late 1950s. His heartfelt, energized style caught the attention of Billy Graham, who attended services to hear him preach. In 1961 the esteemed evangelist hired Thielman to work for him at Montreat Presbyterian Church. — *Deena C. Bouknight*

Divine Inspiration
BASILICA OF ST. LAWRENCE

Compared in opulence to the loftiest cathedrals in Europe, Basilica of St. Lawrence in Asheville owes its uncommon beauty and architectural ingenuity to a famous architect wanting to attend Mass in July 1905. Having gained international acclaim for his building method that allowed for great flexibility in design, Spanish-born Rafael Guastavino had come to Asheville in the mid-1890s to help with the construction of Biltmore Estate. When he tried to attend Mass at the local Catholic church, the crowd of summer visitors prohibited him from finding a seat. After the service, he approached the priest and offered to design a more spacious church that would "offer ample seating for strangers."

The priest sent out 3,000 letters around the country soliciting donations, with only three refusals. Construction began soon after — the congregation helping to lay the massive stone foundation. Other than its brick walls, the entire structure is built of Guastavino tile vaulting. There are no wooden or steel beams. In 1908, as construction was nearly complete, Guastavino died unexpectedly; he is buried in a crypt inside the church. His son, Rafael Jr., helped finish the project.

Walking into Guastavino's creation — through the enormous carved doors and beneath a central statue of Saint Lawrence — is breathtaking. The free-standing elliptical dome on the sanctuary *(above, top left)* appears to have no support. Complementing the architecture is a dazzling display of large stained-glass windows, impressive Italian marble statues of saints, a hand-carved Spanish walnut crucifixion tableau *(above, lower right)*, and an 1,800-pound Tennessee marble altar table. The sacristy door is adorned with a carving titled *Pastor Bonus*, which is a representation of the good shepherd *(above, top right)*. In the Lady Chapel rises the marble statue, *The Assumption of Mary*.

For all its beauty, St. Lawrence's contributions as a spiritual institution are stunning as well. Its priests have included the Rev. Louis J. Bour, who passed out bags of 100 pennies to beggars during the Great Depression, and Joseph L. Howze, St. Lawrence's first African-American priest — who became one of the few African-American bishops in the nation.

Another milestone for St. Lawrence was its designation as a minor basilica by Pope John Paul II on April 6, 1993. An outward sign and privilege that comes to a basilica is the honor of displaying the Pontifical seal in a stained-glass window over the door. — *Deena C. Bouknight*

Location: **Asheville, Buncombe County**

Current Church Completed: **1909**

Worship: **Regular Mass**

A Rising Star
FIRST BAPTIST CHURCH

Location: **Asheville, Buncombe County**

Current Church Completed: **1927**

Worship: **Regular Services**

Members of First Baptist Church in Asheville settled joyfully into their domed house of worship in 1927, the dedication ceremony taking place in a sanctuary that had no trouble accommodating 2,000 people. It was quite a milestone for a congregation that got its start in a log cabin 200 years before on the banks of the French Broad River.

The story goes that Douglas Ellington, the church's architect, got the job after submitting a sketch on a paper napkin. He went on to win several other architectural commissions in Asheville, including the City Building, the Asheville High School, and the S&W Cafeteria. All are on the National Register of Historic Places.

Santa Maria del Fiore in Florence, Italy, one of the great cathedrals of Europe, was the inspiration for First Baptist's five-story-high sanctuary and dome. A monumental undertaking, the church contains 3,000 tons of crushed stone, 2,000 tons of concrete, 200 tons of steel (for the dome alone), and a million bricks.

Subtle symbols on the interior and exterior of the church convey many aspects of Christianity. The even-sided cross stands for evangelicalism; squares represent each of the four Gospels; and there is the palm leaf, which symbolizes peace and Christ's ultimate victory over sin.

The path to this remarkable church led through periods of prosperity and economic challenges for the First Baptist congregation. Two years after its completion came the worldwide financial collapse that ushered in the Great Depression. Slowly and steadily, the church held strong, finally becoming debt-free in 1951. — *Deena C. Bouknight*

The Art of Forgiveness
CHAPEL OF THE PRODIGAL

Gaither Chapel, built in 1935, has long been a must-see landmark for visitors to Montreat College, a small, liberal arts school founded in 1916 just north of Black Mountain. It is, after all, where the world's most famous evangelist, the Rev. Billy Graham *(center, in 1962)*, and his wife, Ruth, were married.

Since 1998, however, a second chapel at Montreat has also commanded attention. In fact, the Chapel of the Prodigal *(opposite page, top left)*, featuring the work of renowned artist Ben Long, has become a destination unto itself.

The primary reason is Long's *The Return of the Prodigal (opposite page, top right)*, a 16-by-17-foot fresco that graces the front wall of the chapel. A North Carolina native, Long is probably best-known for his church frescoes in Ashe County. He sailed into uncharted territory with *The Return of the Prodigal* in that it was his first fresco on a wall built to his specifications.

The fresco portrays Jesus' parable of a wayward son who returned home after squandering the inheritance he had demanded from his father. Long's rendering of the homecoming depicts the father joyfully embracing the young man — a powerful symbol of God's unconditional love and forgiveness.

Although the fresco is unquestionably the centerpiece of the Chapel of the Prodigal, it is by no means its only asset. The 212-seat chapel, rendered in local stone, is topped by a magnificent 85-foot steeple. The interior features heavy, rustic timbers that make up the sanctuary's roof trusses and mosaic tile designed to represent a Celtic cross *(opposite page, lower right)*.

Also of interest is the Ruth Bell Graham Prayer Room, featuring a hand-forged iron cross *(opposite page, lower left)*, a kneeling bench, and wall calligraphy that reads, "Come Unto Me." Mrs. Graham selected the words from Matthew 11:28 as an invitation to those who come to pray. The prayer room and the steeple honor Mrs. Graham, a trustee emerita at Montreat College, and were gifts from the Billy Graham Evangelistic Association. — *Jimmy Tomlin*

Location: **Montreat College, Montreat, Buncombe County**

Chapel Completed: **1998**

Worship: **Open Daily to Visitors**

The Kindness of Strangers
TOE RIVER FREE WILL BAPTIST CHURCH

Location: **Huntdale, Mitchell County**

Current Church Completed: **1900**

Worship: **Regular Services**

In the yellowing pages of its church book, records of the Toe River Free Will Baptist Church in the high hills of Mitchell County date to 1856. The church, near the confluence of the Toe and Cane rivers, "is about the oldest one around here," noted Betty Tipton, the church clerk, music director, and a Sunday school teacher.

The simple, white frame church was built in 1900, a more bustling era than the rural landscape indicated today. From the church's gabled porch, one can view the Toe River, the railroad track, and the historic Phin Peterson Store.

During those early days, services usually took place monthly. According to Tipton, some folks walked for miles to attend because it was the only time during the month for fellowship, worship — and courtship. Baptisms were, and still are, performed in the river. Preachers kept a close watch on their members, said Tipton. If they did anything wrong or if they missed consecutive services and did not apologize and repent, they were often "turned out indefinitely."

Until the early 1950s, Toe River Free Will stood as a rustic, tin-roofed structure with "rough cracked boards for a floor" and gaps so wide that the ground underneath could be seen. In the winter, one member recalled opening "song books" and laying them over legs to fend off the cold air. A potbellied stove heated the small building; restroom facilities were in the outhouse.

In the 1970s repairs were made to the floor and walls. Then, in the late 1990s, Pineville United Methodist Church near Charlotte took the church on as a mission project. Volunteers raised funds and traveled to Huntdale to expand and modernize the church. In addition to the expansion, member Stacey Johnson created stained-glass windows for the sanctuary, someone else donated a painting of the church in snow, and Betty Tipton stenciled bundles of wheat around the chair railing. The sanctuary received a fresh coat of paint, and the floors were refinished. The outhouse remains as a landmark.

"Those Pineville people were the nicest people I'd ever met," said Tipton. "After they finished our church, they even paid our way to visit their church in Charlotte."

Tipton recorded the details of the expansion project in her history book: "Our Lord is responsible for the completion of this project." Also in Tipton's book is a poem written by Pineville volunteer Pat Claiborne, which reads in part: "… to make their rustic little church more safe, more sure, more sound … now we've friends near old Toe River."

The church sees only about 28 members enter its doors on Sundays. At one time in its past there were more than 100 members. "But a lot of these hollers are not as full of people as they used to be," said Tipton. "Many have moved away or died." Still, Toe River Free Will has never had to close its doors, even in tough times. — *Deena C. Bouknight*

EST. 1900
WELCOME TO TOE RIVER
FREEWILL BAPTIST CHURCH
ASSOC MOTHER CHURCH
PASTOR BILLY BRYANT

The Good Earth
ALL SAINTS EPISCOPAL CHURCH

Nature permeates every fiber of All Saints Episcopal Church — which is exactly what the community of Linville and architect Henry Bacon intended when he began construction of the rustic wonder in 1910.

According to Catherine Morton, great-granddaughter of early Linville developer Hugh MacRae and daughter of Grandfather Mountain President Hugh Morton, "When Bacon got to Linville and saw all the chestnut trees, he decided to use thick chestnut bark siding as his signature style. His architecture affected everything that has been done since in Linville."

Bacon built a few homes in Linville before he was commissioned to design the church. His use of site-available materials led to the inauguration of Linville's sophisticated, bark-clad architecture. He often said, "We'll do the best we can with the materials at hand."

Fortunately for Bacon, one of every four trees in the forests of Linville at the turn of the century was a great American chestnut. Before a blight in the early 20th century decimated American chestnut forests, the massive trees averaged five feet in diameter and their timber was milled into strong, durable lumber.

Bacon's design of All Saints features shingle-style architecture, which incorporates nature's elements and the American Indian technique of using bark for siding — but with the restraint and simplicity of traditional Greek architecture. The sanctuary of the log structure leads worshipers into an enchanted man-made forest of unstripped branches and logs that form an exposed ceiling, the bishop's chair, the altar railing, and the rood screen — which is a divider of medieval origin that separates the congregational area from the service area. The walls are covered inside and out with chestnut bark, as are the ceiling lights.

The church and other structures designed by Bacon in Linville have stood the test of time because of the durability of chestnut bark, which is even more valuable today. As important, the congregation of All Saints has the opportunity to worship in a church built of a native wood that may never be seen again.

In 1913, the same year All Saints was completed, Bacon went on to earn a place in history as architect of the Lincoln Memorial in Washington, D.C. But Catherine Morton believes the architect deserves equal recognition for All Saints. "I put the church one-on-one with the Lincoln Memorial as his best work." — *Deena C. Bouknight*

Location: **Linville, Avery County**

Church Completed: **1913**

Worship: **Services June Through October**

Churches of the Frescoes
ST. MARY'S EPISCOPAL CHURCH
HOLY TRINITY EPISCOPAL CHURCH

As the new priest of St. Mary's Episcopal Church in West Jefferson, J. Faulton Hodge was delighted to learn that artist Ben Long was offering to install a fresco at his tiny Ashe County church. He had only one question: "What's a fresco?"

Hodge found out soon enough, and so did the rest of North Carolina.

The year was 1973, and Long — who grew up in Statesville — had just returned from Italy where he had been studying fresco painting under master artist Pietro Annigoni. Eager to share the ancient art form in this country, Long offered to paint a fresco for free in a North Carolina church. To his dismay, 16 churches turned him down.

Meanwhile, Hodge had been assigned to the two mission churches that comprise the Parish of the Holy Communion — St. Mary's, a circa-1905 meetinghouse whose membership had dwindled to 13 parishioners, and Holy Trinity Episcopal in neighboring Glendale Springs, which closed in the 1930s and was in disrepair. Hodge needed something to reinvigorate his struggling parish.

The story goes that Hodge and Long met at a dinner party in Blowing Rock in 1973, and when Long learned that his new acquaintance was a priest, he repeated his offer to paint a fresco for free. Hodge had never heard of Long — nor of frescoes — but he told the young artist, "We'll take it!" That's when he added, "What's a fresco?"

Fresco is a method of painting directly onto wet lime plaster. As the plaster dries, the pigments are absorbed, giving the painting a three-dimensional realism that cannot be captured in oil paintings or other traditional art forms.

Long, though he was an unknown at the time, has since played a key role in this country's fresco revival, beginning with his highly acclaimed work at St. Mary's. In 1974, the artist began *Mary Great with Child*. Long is said to have used two models for the powerful piece — his wife, who was pregnant at the time, and a young mountain girl he spied one day, whose face he deemed just right for that of the Virgin Mary. It apparently wasn't until weeks later, after the painting was finished, that Long learned the young model's own name was Mary, too. The fresco earned him the prestigious Leonardo da Vinci International Art Award.

He painted two more frescoes at St. Mary's — *The Mystery of Faith* (1975) and *John the Baptist* (1977) — before going on to paint yet another massive fresco in 1980, *The Last Supper*, at nearby Holy Trinity *(right)*.

The divine combination of art and faith has been a blessing for the churches, attracting thousands of visitors and helping to rekindle their spiritual life. Today, the parish worships at both churches, alternating between the two from month to month. Both churches are open daily free of charge and docents are usually on hand to serve as tour guides. — *Jimmy Tomlin*

St. Mary's Episcopal Church
Location: **West Jefferson**
Ashe County

Holy Trinity Episcopal Church
Location: **Glendale Springs**
Ashe County

Worship: **Services Alternate Monthly Between Churches**

Madonna of the Hills
ST. MARY OF THE HILLS EPISCOPAL CHURCH

Location: **Blowing Rock, Watagua County**

Church Completed: **1921**

Worship: **Regular Services**

It is a legend in Blowing Rock that St. Mary of the Hills Church owes its existence to a lumber baron's gratitude for missing the sailing of the *Titanic*. While it was true that W.W. Stringfellow indeed financed the church's construction, St. Mary's official history tells the true story behind the gesture, and it is heartwarming in its own way. The church was Mrs. Stringfellow's idea — a way to give thanks for her husband's recovery from tuberculosis.

By the early part of the 20th century, Blowing Rock had become a hub for titans of industry seeking a cooler summer clime for their families. Amid the scenic vistas they built estates that reflected wealth and culture. To no one's surprise, the church financed by Stringfellow was designed as a showplace of art.

The church's name itself came from artwork commissioned for it. In 1918, while the building was still three years away from being completed, Stringfellow asked friend and fellow Episcopalian Elliott Daingerfield to create an altarpiece. The artist painted *Madonna of the Hills (above)*, a picturesque mountain scene inspired by the area around his Blowing Rock home and the mountain legend of "Lady Mary" walking across the hills at dawn.

Daingerfield had come to Blowing Rock in 1886 to recover from an illness. Upon arriving in the mountains, he proclaimed, "it seemed like heaven itself." The artwork of Daingerfield's oldest daughter, Marjorie, is also represented at the church. Her bronze sculpture of the *Madonna and Child (right)* was unveiled in the Mary Garden in 1972 and is considered one of her best religious works.

Complementing Daingerfield's painting are the *14 Stations of the Cross*, sculpted in 2002 by Alex Hallmark. The self-taught sculptor first did the Annunciation for one of the church's entrance gables. "This gave me the courage to take on the Stations of the Cross," he said. — *Deena C. Bouknight*

"A Time to Every Purpose" — *Ecclesiastes 3:1*
CHURCH OF THE LITTLE FLOWER

Time and chance have been true friends to Church of the Little Flower, a small Catholic chapel in Revere, a rural hamlet of Marshall. Catholicism came to the Madison County community in the early 1900s when Larcy Norton visited relatives in Iowa and, learning of the faith, shared its message in the North Carolina mountains.

A Catholic mission was established, and the group began holding services in one another's homes. With a priest from Hot Springs usually presiding, Mass took place on kitchen tables or dressers, baptisms over sinks. In 1931, the small congregation built its own church — a simple cedar shake building with a bell tower, named after St. Therese of the Little Flower.

Notable among the priests who served Little Flower was Andrew Graves, who cared for the needs of the church for more than 50 years. He made regular trips to New York and Washington, D.C., to gather much-needed shoes and coats for residents and to raise funds to support his mission. Recalled Sue Vilcinskas, who was married in the chapel, "He taught us about life, love, and living."

When Graves' health declined and he could no longer conduct regular services, membership waned. In the 1980s, visiting priests came sporadically until the doors finally closed.

In the 1990s, Carl Mumpower, a member of the Asheville City Council, bought the farmland on which the dilapidated building stood. He planned to restore it and convert it into a cottage, "but when I started renovating it, I realized what a gem I had here. It's a little unusual for a Catholic church to be out here in the middle of nowhere. I wanted this precious little church to continue to have a life."

Mumpower's handiwork breathed new life into the structure. He restored the wood floors, painted, and opened the church's doors to a second chance. People now use it for weddings and gatherings. Curious travelers stop here to rest and admire the little chapel. At least once a month and on special occasions a Catholic service is performed.

Treasured spiritual icons abound in the church, many from its early days: statues of the Virgin Mary and St. Therese, a wooden cross holding the body of Jesus, and a silver cross blessed by Pope John Paul II. — *Deena C. Bouknight*

Location: **Revere, Madison County**

Church Completed: **1931**

Worship: **Mass Held Once a Month; Open to Visitors and for Special Occasions**

Hope Springs Eternal
ST. JUDE'S CHAPEL OF HOPE

In the mountains of Madison County, there stands a humble chapel designed not so much as a house of worship — though it certainly is that, too — but more as an expression of gratitude.

Measuring 12 feet by 16 feet, St. Jude's Chapel of Hope will never command the attention of the state's larger, more majestic chapels. No pipe organ, marble columns, or Renaissance paintings to take your breath away. Nor does St. Jude's have a rich, reverential history, considering it was built only in 1990.

So why does this small, unobtrusive wayside chapel inspire such awe for those who come here to behold its simple sanctuary, and perhaps to meet with God during their visit? Ah, now here is a story that will take your breath away.

St. Jude's Chapel of Hope stands in a wooded area along Spring Creek, near where state highways 63 and 209 intersect. The nondenominational chapel was built by Beverly Barutio, who settled in Spring Creek in 1983 with her husband, Bill. In 1981 Beverly was diagnosed with non-Hodgkin's lymphoma, and doctors offered little hope for her long-term survival. While undergoing chemotherapy, Beverly — a devout Catholic — prayed to St. Jude, the patron saint of desperate situations and seemingly hopeless causes. She vowed if she were healed, she would build a chapel dedicated to St. Jude and to God.

Beverly's prayers were answered. The cancer went into remission, and her health thrived for the better part of 20 years.

And Beverly made good on her promise. In 1990, she and Bill built the small chapel with stained-glass windows and named it St. Jude's Chapel of Hope, in honor of her miraculous recovery. A sign out front quotes Psalm 121:1 — "I will lift up mine eyes unto the hills from whence cometh my help" — and invites visitors to "stop — rest — reflect." A stream runs beside the chapel.

About 10,000 people visit the chapel each year — and weddings and funerals have been held here, too — but the chapel does not hold regular worship services. For one thing, it seats only eight people. More important, though, Beverly always saw the sanctuary as just that — a place of rest where passers-by could take refuge from the crazy world around them. She saw it as a place to draw near to God and as such, she kept the chapel open around the clock.

The Barutios eventually moved away. Beverly died in 2002, at age 66 — years after her bleak prognosis — and her ashes were scattered in the stream by the chapel.

Beverly's legacy to this community — and to all who pass through — remains. St. Jude's still stands on the Barutios' former property, and the new owners keep it open at all time. Every day, visitors come here and find what Beverly found — and what she prayed others would find, too. Peace. — *Jimmy Tomlin*

Location: **Trust, Madison County**

Church Completed: **1990**

Worship: **Open Daily to Visitors**

STOP — REST — REFLECT: "It's very peaceful," reflected Bill Barutio of his wife's streamside chapel. "People say they feel closer to God there than in any other structure they've ever been in."

ACKNOWLEDGMENTS

This book is the culmination of many people's efforts, ideas, vision, and work.

The talented circle of writers who contributed to this book traveled hundreds of miles, interviewed dozens of people, and opened their hearts to find meaningful stories, entertaining tales, and the spiritual essence of each church about which they wrote.

With creativity, skill, and raw perseverance, photographer and friend Mark Wagoner embraced this project; the results of his work take you to more than 80 houses of worship and give this book the essential sense of time and place. Image manager Jill Davis seamlessly coordinated schedules and appointments, and attended to the massive details associated with a photography project of this magnitude. In addition, much appreciation goes to photographers Alan Watson, Matt Hulsman, Ray Matthews, Keith McKenzie, and Bruce Roberts and to illustrator Jane Shasky for their contributions.

Copy editors Betty Work and Amanda Hiatt labored countless hours over the stories included in this volume. Their command of language, constructive criticism, conscientiousness, and enthusiasm refined this project into a polished work of art.

I am grateful to Our State Books executive vice president Lynn Tutterow, production director Cheryl Bissett, products manager Erica Derr, and marketing director Amy Jo Wood for their ideas, attention to detail, and thoughtfulness in shepherding this book from a concept to the printer to the readers' hands.

Art director extraordinaire Larry Williams is credited with wrapping our words in beauty through his elegant design and keen selection of photography. In addition to his rare talent as an artist, his hopefulness, fellowship, and delightful sense of humor make working for Our State Books a dream.

And in the category of dreams coming true, I owe my deepest thanks to Our State publisher and owner Bernie Mann, whose steadfast support, leadership, and friendship through the years have changed and enriched my life immeasurably.

For their guidance, suggestions, and encouragement, I thank special friends D.G. Martin, Cheminne Taylor-Smith, and Bets Woodard. And I owe a tremendous debt to Catherine Bishir, senior architectural historian of Preservation North Carolina, who contributed to our architectural and historical accounts and helped with the difficult process of church selection. This project has benefited greatly from her knowledge and expertise.

Above all, Our State Books wishes to thank all of the churches that graciously opened their doors to us and without whose communities of faith this book would not have been possible. — *Mary Best*

ABOUT THE WRITERS

DEENA C. BOUKNIGHT

Having worked as a magazine editor before becoming a freelance writer, Deena C. Bouknight writes for many local, national, and international publications, including *Our State* magazine. She is the author of *Our Wintry Day Walk*, a book about an experience with her son; several more stories and books are forthcoming. Although she has traveled extensively in Europe — her grandmother was from Luxembourg — the Carolinas are her home. Deena lives in Columbia, South Carolina, with her husband, Gary, and adopted children Justin and Madeline.

DIANE SILCOX-JARRETT

Freelance writer Diane Silcox-Jarrett is the author of two books. *One Woman's Dream* is a biography of African-American educator Charlotte Hawkins Brown; *Heroines of the American Revolution America's Founding Mothers* is a collection of biographies of the women of the American Revolution and their courageous tales. She has also worked in the public information office for the North Carolina state government and is a contributing writer to *Our State* magazine. Diane lives outside of Raleigh with husband Alex and children Daniel and Kimberley.

DAVID LA VERE

A professor of history at the University of North Carolina at Wilmington, David La Vere has been a longtime contributor to the pages of *Our State* magazine, as well as to numerous professional and academic journals. His research specialty is Southern Plains and Southeastern Indians, and he has published four books related to his area of expertise, including *Contrary Neighbors: The Southern Plains and the Removed Indians in Indian Territory*, which won the 2001 Oklahoma Book Award for Non-Fiction.

KEITH MCKENZIE

Although a newcomer to the professional freelance-writing market, North Carolina native Keith McKenzie has had a penchant for writing, especially short stories, since he was a young boy. He graduated from Baylor University with a degree in philosophy and has dabbled in a variety of professions, which he says makes him "feel as if I am a connoisseur of the American working place." But, he "always approached the marketplace like a writer looking for material." He and wife Oksana live in Greensboro.

JIMMY TOMLIN

Statesville native Jimmy Tomlin has more than 20 years of journalism experience. Currently, he works as a feature writer and columnist for the *High Point Enterprise*. He also is a freelance contributor to a variety of regional and national publications, including *Our State* magazine. He has received numerous state and national writing awards, including first place in the 2003 Amy Writing Awards, a competition that honors biblical truth in writing. Jimmy and his wife, Becky, live in Greensboro and have two daughters, Ashley and Caroline.

KATHY GRANT WESTBROOK

With a broad educational background ranging from transportation management to education to geology, Four Oaks resident Kathy Grant Westbrook writes on a variety of subjects for numerous publications, including *Our State* magazine and *New Homes and Ideas* magazine. She and her husband, Steve, enjoy traveling and are members of Four Oaks United Methodist Church.

BIBLIOGRAPHY

Bishir, Catherine W., and Michael T. Southern. *A Guide to the Historic Architecture of Eastern North Carolina*. Chapel Hill, N.C.: University of North Carolina Press, 1996.

Bishir, Catherine W., and Michael T. Southern. *A Guide to the Historic Architecture of Piedmont North Carolina*. Chapel Hill, N.C.: University of North Carolina Press, 2003.

Bishir, Catherine W., and Michael T. Southern. *A Guide to the Historic Architecture of Western North Carolina*. Chapel Hill, N.C.: University of North Carolina Press, 1999.

Butler, Jon, Grant Wacker, and Randall Balmer. *Religion in American Life*. New York: Oxford University Press, 2003.

Chiat, Marilyn J. *America's Religious Architecture: Sacred Places for Every Community*. New York: John Wiley & Sons, 1997.

Hudson, Winthrop S. *Religion in America*. New York: Charles Scribner's Sons, 1973.

Powell, William S. *North Carolina Through Four Centuries*. Chapel Hill, N.C.: University of North Carolina Press, 1989.

Russell, Anne, and Marjorie Megivern. *North Carolina Portraits of Faith: A Pictorial History of Religions*. Norfolk, Va.: Donning, 1986.

Wilson, Charles Reagan, and William Ferris, eds. *Encyclopedia of Southern Culture*. Chapel Hill, N.C.: University of North Carolina Press, 1989.

PHOTO CREDITS

ALL PHOTOGRAPHY BY MARK WAGONER EXCEPT FOR THE FOLLOWING:

page 26: Ray Matthews

page 27: Ray Matthews

page 37: Alan Watson

page 39: Alan Watson

page 39: Alan Watson

page 40: Alan Watson

page 52: Bruce Roberts

page 53: Bruce Roberts

page 79: Ray Matthews

pages 98-99: Les Todd/Duke University Photography

page 112: Alan Watson

page 113: Alan Watson

page 117: Matt Hulsman

page 156: courtesy of Wake Forest University

page 169: courtesy of Emmett Forrest

page 26: courtesy of Keith McKenzie

page 203: Bruce Roberts

page 209: Alan Watson

INDEX *of* CHURCHES

Grove Presbyterian,
611 South Main Street,
Kenansville, Duplin County, 60

Hannah's Creek Primitive
Baptist, U.S. Highway 301 South,
Four Oaks, Johnston County, 84

Holland's United Methodist,
9433 Ten Ten Road, Raleigh,
Wake County, 104

Holy Trinity Episcopal,
120 Glendale School Road,
Glendale Springs,
Ashe County, 208

Home Moravian,
529 South Church Street, Winston-
Salem, Forsyth County, 158

Hopewell Presbyterian,
10500 Beatties Ford Road,
Huntersville, Mecklenburg
County, 128

Little Tabernacle,
West Street, Falcon,
Cumberland County, 112

Luola's Chapel,
Orton Plantation, 9149 Orton
Road S.E., Winnabow,
Brunswick County, 48

Mariah's Chapel,
Grandin Road, Grandin (near
Lenoir), Caldwell County, 172

Milton Presbyterian,
66 Broad Street, Milton,
Caswell County, 90

Old Bluff Presbyterian,
Old Bluff Church Road, Wade,
Cumberland County, 110

Our Lady of Grace,
2205 West Market Street,
Greensboro, Guilford County, 140

Philadelphus Presbyterian,
1518 Buie-Philadelphus Road,
Red Springs, Robeson County, 56

Piney Woods Friends Meeting,
Piney Woods Road, Belvidere,
Perquimans County, 26

Pleasant Ridge United Church
of Christ, 2049 Pleasant Ridge
Road, Greensboro, Guilford
County, 146

Post Chapels,
Fort Bragg, Cumberland
County, 118

Prospect United Methodist,
3929 Missouri Road, Prospect
(near Pembroke),
Robeson County, 58

Providence United Methodist,
139 Main Street, Swan Quarter,
Hyde County, 32

Queen Street Methodist,
500 North Queen Street,
Kinston, Lenoir County, 62

Republican Baptist,
1300 Republican Road,
Republican (near Windsor),
Bertie County, 78

Rock Springs Camp Meeting
Ground, Campground Road,
Denver, Lincoln County, 178

Sandy Creek Baptist,
4765 Sandy Creek Church Road,
Liberty, Randolph County, 148

Sandy Creek Primitive Baptist,
4785 Sandy Creek Church Road,
Liberty, Randolph County, 148

Shiloh Methodist,
Shiloh Woods Road, Troy,
Montgomery County, 124

Soldiers Memorial A.M.E. Zion,
306 North Church Street,
Salisbury, Rowan County, 130

St. James Episcopal,
25 South 3rd Street, Wilmington,
New Hanover County, 44

St. John's Episcopal,
302 Green Street, Fayetteville,
Cumberland County, 114

St. John's Episcopal,
Williamsboro Road,
Williamsboro, Vance County, 86

St. Jude's Chapel of Hope,
N.C. Highways 63 and 209,
Trust, Madison County, 214

St. Mary's Episcopal,
400 Beaver Creek School Road,
West Jefferson County, 208

St. Mary of the Hills Episcopal,
140 Chestnut Drive, Blowing
Rock, Watauga County, 210

St. Matthew's Episcopal,
210 Saint Marys Road,
Hillsborough, Orange County, 94

St. Paul's Episcopal,
101 West Gale Street, Edenton,
Chowan County, 28

St. Paul's Episcopal,
200 West Cowles Street,
Wilkesboro, Wilkes County, 170

St. Philips Moravian,
911 South Church Street,
Winston-Salem,
Forsyth County, 160

St. Thomas Episcopal,
Craven Street, Bath,
Beaufort County, 36

Toe River Free Will Baptist,
1334 Huntdale Road, Huntdale
(near Green Mountain),
Mitchell County, 204

Tucker's Grove Camp Meeting
Grounds, State Road 1360 and
N.C. Highway 73, Machpelah (near
Lincolnton), Lincoln County, 178

Union Grove Amish,
Hunting Creek Church
Road, Hamptonville,
Yadkin County, 164

Village Chapel,
Bald Head Island,
Brunswick County, 52

Village Chapel,
Village Green, N.C. Highway 2,
Pinehurst, Moore County, 122

Wait Chapel,
Wake Forest University, Winston-
Salem, Forsyth County, 156

Waldensian Presbyterian,
109 East Main Street, Valdese,
Burke County, 174

Zion (Organ) Lutheran,
1515 Organ Church Road,
Rockwell, Rowan County, 132

Founded in 2003, Our State Books celebrates North Carolina's lively culture, natural beauty, and rich heritage by publishing books that exemplify the Tar Heel experience. Our readers — loyal, astute, and with a keen eye for detail and superior writing — expect works of unparalleled quality on subjects of interest to those who live in, visit, or simply cherish the Old North State.

Our State Books is a division of Mann Media, publisher of *Our State* magazine. Continually published since 1933, *Our State* is North Carolina's only monthly travel, history, and folklore publication and is enjoyed by more than half a million readers each month. Our State Books evolved from our readers' desire to learn more about their adored home state in a photographically intensive, friendly, and intelligent manner.

On average, Our State Books releases three to four original books a year and employs many of the same writers and photographers who have made *Our State* magazine one of the most successful regional magazines in the nation. Subject areas include North Carolina general-interest nonfiction, travel, culture, history, religion, gardening, nature, art and architecture, essays and memoirs, food, and photography.

Recent titles include *North Carolina Lighthouses: A Tribute of History and Hope* by Cheryl Shelton-Roberts and Bruce Roberts and *Sweet Tea, Fried Chicken, and Lazy Dogs: Reflections on North Carolina Life* by Bill Thompson.

AMEN.